A New Approach to
Sight Singing

A New Approach to
Sight Singing

SIXTH EDITION

Sol Berkowitz
Gabriel Fontrier
Leo Kraft
Perry Goldstein
Edward Smaldone

W. W. NORTON & COMPANY *New York / London*

W. W. Norton & Company has been independent since its founding in 1923, when William Warder Norton and Mary D. Herter Norton first published lectures delivered at the People's Institute, the adult education division of New York City's Cooper Union. The Nortons soon expanded their program beyond the Institute, publishing books by celebrated academics from America and abroad. By mid-century, the two major pillars of Norton's publishing program—trade books and college texts—were firmly established. In the 1950s, the Norton family transferred control of the company to its employees, and today—with a staff of four hundred and a comparable number of trade, college, and professional titles published each year—W. W. Norton & Company stands as the largest and oldest publishing house owned wholly by its employees.

Editor: Justin Hoffman
Editorial Assistant: Grant Phelps
Managing Editor, College: Marian Johnson
Managing Editor, College Digital Media: Kim Yi
Project Editor: David Bradley
Copyeditor: Elizabeth Bortka
Production Manager: Sean Mintus
Marketing Manager, Music: Trevor Penland
Composition and layout: Jouve
Manufacturing: LSC Kendallville

Permission to use copyrighted material is included in the credits section of this book, which begins on page 435.

Library of Congress Cataloging-in-Publication Data

Names: Berkowitz, Sol. | Fontrier, Gabriel. | Kraft, Leo. | Goldstein, Perry,
    1952- | Smaldone, Edward M.
Title: A new approach to sight singing / Sol Berkowitz, Gabriel Fontrier, Leo
    Kraft, Perry Goldstein, Edward Smaldone.
Description: 6th edition. | New York : W. W. Norton & Company, [2017] |
    Includes index.
Identifiers: LCCN 2017012513 | ISBN 9780393284911 (spiral)
Subjects: LCSH: Sight-singing.
Classification: LCC MT870.B485 N5 2017 | DDC 783/.0423—dc23 LC record available at
https://lccn.loc.gov/2017012513

W. W. Norton & Company, Inc., 500 Fifth Avenue, New York, NY 10110
www.wwnorton.com
W. W. Norton & Company, Ltd., 15 Carlisle Street, London W1D 3BS

3 4 5 6 7 8 9 0

Contents

Preface to the Sixth Edition

A New Approach to Sight Singing consists of musical materials specifically composed for the study of sight singing, now presented alongside classical and folk melodies. A mastery of sight singing is essential to the performer, the scholar, the composer, the teacher—to any professional musician or well-trained amateur. This text helps students master sight singing skills with carefully paced exercises that introduce new musical complexities at a controlled pace, systematically increasing in difficulty. This combination of melodies composed specifically for the text and melodies from the literature allows for an ideal pedagogical progression.

Organization

A New Approach to Sight Singing consists of four chapters, as well as supplementary exercises and two appendices. Chapter One contains unaccompanied melodies and forms the core of the book. Chapter Two consists of unpitched rhythm exercises. Chapter Three presents vocal duets, while Chapter Four contains Sing and Play exercises—melodies with piano accompaniment. The supplementary exercises contain specific drills in scales and chords, chromatic notes of all kinds, and advanced harmonic problems. Appendix I is an expanded glossary of musical terms used in the text. Appendix II explains some frequently used musical symbols.

Each chapter (except Chapter One) has four sections, consistent with a four-semester musicianship sequence. Section I is at the elementary level, Sections II and III intermediate, and Section IV advanced. Section V of Chapter One—covering post-tonal melodies—may be used in the third and fourth semesters of a four-semester sequence concurrently with Sections III and IV, or in the last semester, concurrently with Section IV only. Each section corresponds to one semester of an undergraduate course. The material of each section is graded progressively, and corresponding sections of each chapter are designed to be worked through simultaneously.

The melodies in Chapter One, Section I introduce musical topics progressively: while the first tunes are simple and quite short, later ones gradually increase in length and complexity. These melodies are diatonic, emphasizing fundamental aspects of tonality. Stepwise motion, skips based on familiar chord outlines, the practice of certain intervals, and basic rhythmic patterns are presented here.

The melodies of Section II, while largely diatonic, introduce a few chromatic notes, as well as simple modulation, altered chords, larger skips, and somewhat more complex rhythms. This section also targets additional intervals for practice. Modal melodies also appear in this section.

Section III includes more chromaticism and additional modulation. Melodies are longer, phrase structures more complex, and rhythms more diverse. Section IV offers more challenging exercises in tonality as well as in rhythm, meter, and phrasing; dynamics, phrase structure, and musical interpretation are on a more sophisticated level. Section V introduces a progressive method for developing skills in post-tonal music, systematically expanding the vocabulary of intervals. Beginning only with seconds, the next part expands the vocabulary to perfect fourths, then perfect fifths, and continues on in that fashion until all simple intervals are introduced. Students spend enough time with the limited number of intervals to get them in their ears before moving on. The melodies represent music composed in different styles, including exercises in the last three parts composed using serial techniques.

Chapter Two isolates rhythm. This chapter is best used in conjunction with each new rhythmic and metrical offering in Chapter One, and as a way for students to become more comfortable with various meters and durations before applying them to the pitched material.

Chapter Three develops skill in ensemble singing. Students not only sing their own part but also listen to another, sung by a different voice. This introduces performance issues raised when collaborating sensitively with others in making music: singing together, in tune, and in a musical manner. The exercises may be given as prepared assignments, and are equally useful as unprepared assignments in class. Students typically sing their lines individually, followed by the same two students singing their lines together before the class sings the two lines together.

Experience has strengthened our conviction that the piano is essential in developing musicianship. Chapter Four affords opportunities to develop that musicianship by playing one part and singing another. In doing so, students improve musical independence while also developing good intonation and sharpening rhythmic skills. Chapter Four also offers an effective way to study the relationship between harmony and melody. While the instructor may ask students to perform Sing and Play exercises at sight, these will most often be given as homework.

The Sixth Edition

With this new Sixth Edition of *A New Approach to Sight Singing*, we've made some significant changes in response to feedback we've received. In the previous editions, Chapter One contained melodies, composed by the authors, that systematically introduced music of increasing difficulty. With this approach, the text proceeds at a steady pace, ensuring that students have enough time to develop each skill. The most significant change in the Sixth Edition is the inclusion of about one hundred melodies from the literature, integrated into Chapter One. The book now offers the best of both worlds: melodies composed specifically to systematically train students in sight singing and excellent melodies from the literature.

Other changes in the Sixth Edition include:

- Substantially revised Sing and Play exercises, where the piano parts are playable by students with a variety of keyboard skill levels.
- Comprehensively revised materials on posttonal aural skills and rhythm that were added in the fifth edition. Pacing is improved in this sixth edition.
- Expanded use of roman numerals, showing the harmonic basis for melodies. These roman numerals can be used to improvise accompaniments to melodies and to help students understand the harmonic implications of sight singing.

A Typical Class

In most curricula, sight singing is coordinated with dictation. Courses might mix unprepared sight singing with singing prepared exercises. (We suggest devoting one day per week to prepared exercises.) Preparation of melodies teaches students how to prepare polished "performances" of melodies and strengthens their skills in solfège or other systems that associate words or numbers with pitches. Unprepared sight singing, and especially its practice by students, strengthens students' ability to "hear" a melody spontaneously and to truly sing at sight. Sight singing duets engages students and practices skills necessary for the development of skilled performance.

Much of the class time will probably be devoted to singing solo melodies, which comprise almost half of the book. But frequent use of Chapters Two, Three, and Four offers variety to engage students while improving various skills. Instructors may also choose to incorporate the Sing and Play assignments in Chapter Four by having students record assigned performances and submit them electronically.

Some institutions teach musicianship as part of the theory curriculum, integrating the study of musicianship into the study of theory; others separate the two areas. *A New Approach to Sight Singing* is organized so that it may be adapted to different programs of study. Sections I and II of each chapter may be integrated with the study of diatonic harmony and counterpoint, while Sections III and IV may be coordinated with the study of chromatic harmony, and Section V with the study of post-tonal music.

This book offers a large body of materials, so much so that it would be impossible for even the most rigorous program to incorporate all of it. With plenty of material to choose from, both for preparation and for singing at sight, instructors may choose the kinds of exercises (solos, duets, Sing and Play, etc.) and the exercises themselves that best suit their programs' needs. Weekly assignments might include the preparation of melodies in major and minor keys, in several clefs, emphasizing different aspects of theory (for example, arpeggiation of the dominant, tonicization of the supertonic), stressing lyrical singing, running sixteenth notes for the mastery of solfège, in short, chosen with an eye to the development of a diverse and complete set of skills. The explicit introduction of harmonic concepts and materials (altered chords such as the Neapolitan6 and augmented sixths, tonicization of various keys, etc.) can be used to reinforce concepts learned in music theory and bring them to aural life.

As an aid to organizing the course, the specific skills to be obtained that are introduced in Chapter One are identified by brief headings, each followed by a short group of melodies that focuses on the topic at hand. Immediately after, there is a longer group of melodies combining many topics introduced to that point.

Recommendations for Further Study

Those wishing to find a way of developing better musicianship skills outside the classroom may consult Leo Kraft's *A New Approach to Ear Training*. An excellent way for students to work on their own is to write down, daily, phrases of melodies that they know (but haven't seen) in order to become more facile at translating melody into notation. It is also valuable to play familiar music by ear on the piano or another instrument. In addition, there are now numerous websites that allow students to work on musicianship skills outside of the classroom, including InQuizitive for Aural Skills—a formative, adaptive system for developing aural skills that may be packaged with this text.

Acknowledgments

We take this opportunity to express our appreciation and thanks to the many generations of students, undergraduate and graduate, at Queens College and Stony Brook University, whose responses to this book have helped shape our thinking and who have taught us so much about how good sight singing skills are acquired. We are indebted to the practical experience of the folks on the ground—the dedicated faculty and teaching assistants at Queens College and Stony Brook University. We also are grateful to our colleagues around the country who read the proposals and reviewed previous editions and made so many valuable suggestions for the Fifth and Sixth editions. Reviewers for the Sixth Edition included Michael Berry (University of Washington), Martin Blessinger (Texas Christian University), Mark Conley (University of Rhode Island), Murray Gross (Alma College), Matthew Herman (Western Kentucky University), Jeffrey Kresky (William Paterson University), Jeffrey Lovell (Lebanon Valley College), Steven Reale (Youngstown State University), Nico Schüler (Texas State University), Ann Stimson (The Ohio State University), and Barbara Wallace (Dallas Baptist University). For the Fifth Edition, reviewers included Michael Baker (University of Kentucky), Martin Blessinger (Texas Christian University), Susan Kenney (Brigham Young University), Mark Mazzatenta (High Point University), Raina Murnak (University of Miami), Ruth Rendleman (Montclair State University), Eva Sze (New York University), Gregory Wanamaker (Crane School of Music, SUNY–Potsdam), and Craig Weston (Kansas State University).

Thanks are due to Professor John Castellini, the patient and devoted editor of the first four editions, who continuously labored with the manuscript and helped define the book's final form. Many of the ideas concerning music and music theory were gained during the original authors' years as students and colleagues of Karol Rathaus. For the Fifth Edition, we are indebted to editor Maribeth Payne, for trusting us to maintain the same high standards that characterize the first four editions and who provided invaluable advice. For the day-to-day editing, and for her advice, encouragement, and unabated sense of humor, Courtney Hirschey was a joy to work with on the Fifth Edition. We are equally grateful to Justin Hoffman, the trusty editor of the Sixth Edition, for his excellent advice and encouragement, and for rallying us when time seemed to permit little opportunity to produce the manuscript in time for publication. David Bradley was project editor, Sean Mintus managed production, Elizabeth Bortka copyedited the manuscript, Peter Stanley Martin proofread the text and musical examples, Eric B. Chernov created the index, Trevor Penland handled marketing, and Grant Phelps was editorial assistant. We'd like to express our thanks to our wives, Karen Smaldone and Dawn Stonebraker, for creating the warm and encouraging environment that allowed us to complete this edition.

▨   ▨   ▨

Everyone can learn to sing and to enjoy singing. No matter what kind of voice one possesses, compe-tence in singing can be achieved by consistent practice. The satisfactions thus gained will more than justify the effort expended. To be sure, sight singing is not an end in itself: it opens the door to musical experiences of many kinds. The goal of training in sight singing is not to develop great singing talent (though it will certainly aid the amateur and professional singer); rather, by singing, we outwardly manifest our ability to hear music in our mind's ear. Music does not live on paper. To bring it to life, there must be an instrument that can sing, an ear that can hear, and a musical mind that can sing and hear in the silence of thought.

Berkowitz/Fontrier/Kraft, 1995
Goldstein/Smaldone, 2016

※ CHAPTER ONE ※

Melodies

Before singing a melody (or performing music of any sort) the singer must understand thoroughly the system of music notation we use today. The five-line staff with the clef signs, time signatures, tempo indications, and expression markings constitute a musical code, all the elements of which must be decoded simultaneously in order to transform what has been set down on paper into music.

Establish the Key

The melodies in Section I are tonal. Each is written in a specific key and the student must establish that key before attempting to sing. The tonic note of the key (rather than the first note of the melody) should be played on the piano or the pitch pipe and sung by the student. Then the scale of the key should be sung, ascending and descending, after which an arpeggio consisting of tonic, 3rd, 5th, and octave may be sung to establish further a feeling for the tonality of the melody. (Specific tips for the sight singing of post-tonal music are given prior to Section V.)

Establish the Tempo

Next it is necessary to determine the tempo (rate of speed) and the meter (number of beats to the measure). Many different tempo indications have been used in this book to familiarize the student with most of the terms in common use. It is important that the singer know the meaning of these tempo markings, all of which are to be found in the Glossary (p. 430).

The time signature denotes meter. Simple meters (duple, triple, and quadruple) are indicated by signatures having a 2, 3, or 4 as the upper numeral, or by the signs **C** (common time, corresponding to $\frac{4}{4}$ meter) or **¢** (*alla breve* or cut time, corresponding to $\frac{2}{2}$

meter). Regular compound meters ($\frac{6}{8}$, $\frac{9}{8}$, and $\frac{12}{8}$) typically treat the dotted quarter as the beat.

Tempo can be established and meter defined by beating time as a conductor does. Standard conducting patterns should be used consistently. $\frac{6}{8}$ time may be conducted in six or in two beats; $\frac{9}{8}$ and $\frac{12}{8}$ time in separate beats or in three or four beats respectively. Tempo, and often the character of a melody, will serve the student in determining how to conduct compound meters. For the purposes of this text, it will suffice to conduct using standard patterns of 2, 3, and 4. We give those conducting patterns on p. 2, and the time signature with which they are to be used.

Singing Melodies without Texts

Singing some definite syllable for every note allows the singer to control quality and intonation. In many foreign countries solfège (the application of the *sol-fa* syllables to the degrees of the scale) is used in sight singing. This practice is officially sanctioned by foreign national conservatories. In the United States, however, several methods of singing melodies without texts are in common use. These may be summarized as follows:

Fixed *Do*

In the fixed *do* system, our notes, C, D, E, F, G, A, and B, are called *do*, *re*, *mi*, *fa*, *sol*, *la*, and *ti*. In singing a melody, the name for each note is sung without regard to any accidental. Countries that use this technique have been quite successful with it, perhaps because of the rigorous early training their students receive.

Movable *Do*

In the movable *do* system, *do* always represents the tonic or first degree of the scale, regardless of

1

In two: $\frac{2}{4}$, $\frac{6}{8}$, ¢, $\frac{6}{4}$, and $\frac{5}{8}$

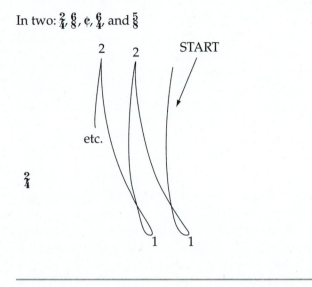

In three: $\frac{3}{4}$, $\frac{9}{8}$, $\frac{3}{2}$, and $\frac{7}{8}$

In four: $\frac{4}{4}$ and $\frac{12}{8}$

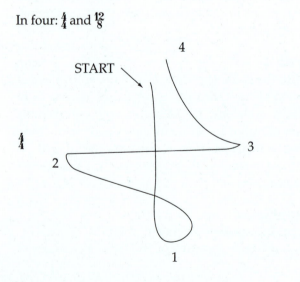

key. Accidentals are accounted for by changing the syllables. The ascending chromatic scale reads as follows: *do, di, re, ri, mi, fa, fi, sol, si, la, li, ti, do*. The descending chromatic scale reads as follows: *do, ti, te, la, le, sol, se, fa, mi, me, re, ra, do*.

When a melody modulates, the new tonic is called *do*, and the other notes of the scale are re-named accordingly. The purpose of this system is to emphasize the relationship between the degrees of the scale, and to develop a feeling for tonality even when the tonal center shifts.

Other Methods

Numbers (1, 2, 3, etc.) may be used instead of syllables (*do, re, mi*, etc.). The application is the same as in the movable *do* system except that there is no numeral change for chromatic tones.

One syllable, such as *la*, may be used for all pitches. Thus the singer does not have to translate the pitch names into syllables or numbers.

A musician is expected to know the system in common use wherever he or she may be; therefore, the student should master more than one of these techniques.

Phrasing

Avoid note-to-note singing, and instead make a genuine effort to grasp an entire phrase as a musical entity. To guide and encourage this process of looking ahead, slurs and articulation markings have been placed over the phrases of every melody. These indications define the phrase structure and serve as a guide to breathing.

Musical Values

In practicing the singing of melodies, as in practicing an instrument, the beginner may be tempted to concentrate on producing the correct pitch, hoping that other musical values will be acquired in due course. But melodies do not exist without rhythm; they also have nuances of dynamics and tempo, and climaxes. These qualities are an integral part of the music. It is possible to improve one's musicianship while learn-ing the technique of sight singing by thinking about musical values with the first melody in the book. As an aid to intelligent and sensitive performance we have included dynamics, expression, and articulation markings throughout the book. The eye should be trained to observe them; the mind to implement them.

Prepare to Sing

The first melodies should be studied carefully in order to develop good musical habits. The student should sing a melody several times, if necessary, until ease and fluency are achieved.

Before you start to sing, we suggest that you:

- Look at the melody quickly (scan it): where are the high and low points?
- Look for dynamic marks and articulation.
- Sing an arpeggio that fits the range of the melody.
- Sing one or more of the warm-ups offered in the Supplementary Exercises at the back of the book in the key and tempo of the exercise.
- Beat time as you sing, using standard conducting patterns (see p. 2).

Practice Tips

A few useful tools will assist you in singing accurately. First, tonic must be kept in mind, and you should be able to reproduce the tonic at any moment within a melody. Tonic is a musical "north star," a way of navigating the scale with constant reference to a fixed point. For example, it is far easier to sing the leading tone in relation to a remembered tonic than it is to sing a difficult interval—say, scale degree six down to the leading tone. Similarly, it may be easier to sing a second or a third in relation to a remembered tonic than to sing large intervals, especially descending ones. It is also useful to remember that melodies, especially good ones, often have an internal logic and a "skeletal" structure that involves half steps and whole steps. In other words, although adjacent notes may involve large intervallic leaps, there may be a step-wise relationship between two notes separated by another. One need only think of the many melodies, for example by J. S. Bach, that have a double structure: notes alternating between two parts of the register that form two coherent lines. The more you understand about the structure of a melody, the better you will become at sight singing. In this regard, you want to develop a good musical memory. An important structural point in a melody may be repeated in the next measure, or start

the next phrase. Remembering what you have just sung, and being aware of repetitions in a melody, or sequences, will help you sing it successfully and understand how the melody is made. Above all, it is important not to think of a melody as a succession of discrete intervals to be sung one interval at a time; this is the least effective way to sight sing. Students and instructors preferring to begin each practice session with warm-up exercises will find appropriate materials among the Supplementary Exercises in the back of the book.

A Practice Regimen

You should plan to set aside 30 minutes daily, five or six days a week, for sight singing practice. The following routine is offered as a guide. Although the exercises may seem very simple at first, following this routine without taking shortcuts will ensure that you develop essential and solid skills of sight singing and syllabic accuracy, which will enable you to move on fluently to more difficult materials.

1. Prepared Sight Singing. Sing through each assigned example five times per practice session. Begin at a steady and comfortable tempo, even if it is slow. During the first two or three days of each week, do the exercise at the piano or another instrument. However, try not to rely on the instrument more than is absolutely necessary. Sing a phrase; if you feel you have gotten off track mid-phrase, play the last note you sang on the piano or another instrument. If you are correct, go on. If not, back up and try again. The less you depend on the piano, the more confidence, accuracy, and skill you will develop. Ideally, you would use the piano only to give the key and starting note, and this will certainly be the case toward the end of your week of practice. After singing through each of the exercises four times, sing the entire sequence of exercises once. Make sure to decrease reliance on the piano as the week goes on.

As you become more comfortable with the exercises, increase your speed to the maximum tempo at which you can still comfortably negotiate pitches, rhythms, syllables, and articulation/dynamic markings. Although tempo markings are provided for each exercise, they are only advisory, a way to suggest the style and mood of the example. You should practice singing exercises with slower markings at a faster tempo, the better to gain facility with solfège. Students who practice consistently with solfège syllables will find such singing "automatic" after only a few weeks. The authors also strongly suggest conducting while singing the exercises (see p. 2). Although this may seem an unnecessary burden while you are also learning to negotiate pitches, rhythm, articulation and dynamics, and solfège syllables, with consistent practice, conducting also will become "automatic."

2. Unprepared Sight Singing. After you have sung through the assigned exercises, spend the rest of your practice time reading through other examples in the book. Choose several exercises and sing each three times, using the piano or an instrument as sparingly as possible. After doing so, move on to other melodies. True sight singing skills—that is, the ability to sound out a melody at sight—can only be developed through practice on melodies one has not learned. One reason for the hundreds of examples in this book is so that you will never run out of melodies to sing at sight.

What to Avoid

For a musician, the ability to "hear" music without playing it is an invaluable tool. Sight singing is an audible way for students to demonstrate that they can accurately translate notation into sound. The ultimate goal of a sight singing curriculum is to develop skills and confidence in "hearing" notation and reproducing that notation through singing. Avoid crutches that enable you to learn and sing a melody but that hinder the growth of your ability to hear and sing music without playing it. Under no circumstances should you learn melodies assigned for prepared sight singing by recording them, or learn them through memorization after several playings at the piano or other instruments. Doing so will not help you learn to hear what you see. Furthermore, you should not write the solfège syllables or numbers into the book, as this will prevent you from gaining facility in the use of syllables or numbers. The well-trained musician will be able to look at a line within a texture and accurately "hear" it without playing it (or anticipate it before playing or singing it), and that goal should be in your mind as you practice.

MELODIES ▨ *SECTION I*

To be used with Section I of all other chapters

The first melodies in this book emphasize the basic aspects of tonality. They are designed to include easily recognizable scale and chordal patterns. These diatonic melodies are based on both major and minor modes.

The phrases are usually symmetrical and short enough to be understood at a glance. However, the diversity of rhythms, keys, modes, tempos, dynamics, and clefs should provide a variety of musical experiences. The treble, bass, and alto clefs are introduced in this section. You should conduct all exercises (see p. 2).

▨ ▨ ▨ The first melodies are based entirely on stepwise motion. The largest range is a single octave. Note values include o 𝅗𝅥 𝅘𝅥 𝅘𝅥𝅘𝅥. (Additional practice in these rhythms may be found in exercises 1–7 in Chapter Two.)

All of these melodies begin with the tonic of the key. Students are encouraged to hear the harmonic implications of the melodies throughout the text. The following melody and several others in Chapter One model roman numeral harmonizations, which you should play at the piano in block chords. (If you have limited keyboard skills, even playing just the root of the appropriate triad in the bass will provide a harmonic reference point.) Harmonizing other melodic exercises (including the duets) as well as transposing this type of exercise are both recommended.

1. *Moderato*

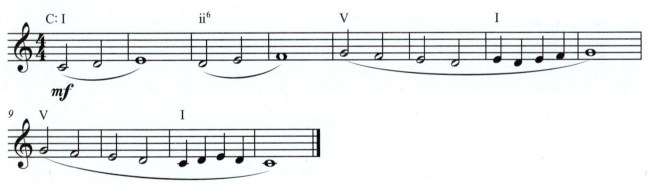

2. *Andante*

3. *Allegretto*

 Conduct cut time in 2. For additional cut time practice, see rhythm exercise 33 and beyond in Chapter Two.

4. *Allegro*

5. *Andante cantabile*

6. *Allegro*

7. *Largo*

8. *Andantino*

9. *Allegretto*

Each of the next three melodies is built in two phrases. Scan the melody for the peak of each phrase.

10. *Con moto*

11. *Allegro*

12. *Allegro deciso*

The pattern of two short phrases and one longer one is found in the next two melodies.

13. *Allegretto*

14. *Andante*

▨ ▨ ▨   The following nine melodies introduce skips in the tonic triad.

15. *Andante con moto*

16. *Vivace*

17. *Allegretto*

18. *Allegro con brio*

19. *Allegro*

20. *Cantabile*

▨ ▨ ▨

The following melodies introduce skips of non-tonic triad notes.

21. *Andante*   **Chorale: "Wie schön leuchtet der Morgenstern"**

22. *Molto allegro*   **Mozart: Symphony No. 13, IV (adapted)**

The rhythm ♩. ♪ is included in the next seven melodies. See rhythm exercises 9, 13, and 22 in Chapter Two.

23. *Allegro*

24. *Allegro moderato*

25. *Allegro*   **Mozart: String Quartet in C, K, 157, I (harmony modified)**

26. *Allegro moderato*

27. *Vivace*

28. *Andante*

29. *Andante*

Three C-minor scales.

Natural

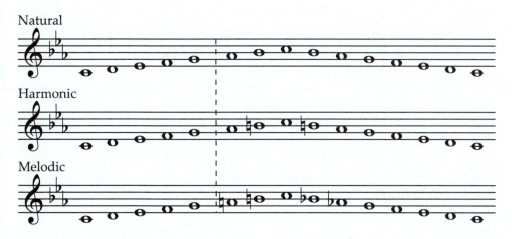

Harmonic

Melodic

Melodies in which the major and minor modes are compared may be found in Supplementary Exercises, p. 415.

The following seven melodies introduce the minor mode. For users of moveable *do*, minor mode melodies incorporate the syllable *me* (pronounced "may") for the third scale degree, and use *le* or *la* for the sixth scale degree and *te* ("tay") or *ti* for the seventh scale degree, depending on the musical situation. The following five melodies are in stepwise motion.

30. *Andante*

31. *Allegro*

32. *Allegro*

33. *Andante*

34. *Allegretto*

The following two melodies contain ascending and descending forms of the melodic minor scale. Note that the sixth and seventh scale degrees are raised as the music ascends to tonic, but not when the scale descends from tonic to the seventh and sixth scale degrees.

35. *Andantino*

36. *Allegro moderato*

37. *Allegro*

38. *Andante cantabile*

Alto Clef

The alto clef can be visualized in relation to the grand staff. The five lines of the alto clef are, in fact, the same as the five middle lines of the grand staff. Thinking of the alto clef in this way ensures not only identifying the correct note but also placing that note in the correct octave.

For the alto clef, the top line is G above middle C, the middle line is middle C, and the bottom line is F below middle C. These additional reference points will make the entire clef easier to master.

    A good way to practice your facility with the alto clef (and later with the tenor clef) is to play melodies on the piano. This reinforces the correct "placement" of the notes of these clefs.

    Another useful trick is to remember that every note is either a line note or a space note. This remains constant in every clef. For example, the D above middle C is a space note, and the E above middle C is a line note, in all seven clefs! This is helpful when you are trying to "see" a familiar note in an unfamiliar clef.

▨ ▨ ▨   Below, the same melody is written in three different clefs.

39a. *Moderato*

39b. *Moderato*

39c. *Moderato*

 The next ten melodies are notated in the alto clef.

40. *Andante*

41. *Largo*

42. *Allegretto*

43. *Allegro con spirito*

44. *Modéré*

The next three melodies should be sung as if notated in the treble, alto, and bass clefs in turn, inserting the needed key signature for each clef. They should also be played at the piano in the register appropriate to each clef. (This exercise can be repeated with any other melodies.)

51. *Allegretto cantabile*

mf

10

52. *Marcato*

f

53. *Andante*

D: I   V⁷   I   ii⁶   V   I

mp   *f*

54. *Moderato con moto*

rall.

p

a tempo

7

pp

Skips in the tonic minor triad are found in the next five minor melodies.

55. *Lento*

p < > < > *mf* > *p*

56. *Andante*

57. *Allegro*

58. *Allegretto*

59. *Moderato*

The next seven melodies include additional rhythmic divisions of the beat in simple meters. Review rhythm exercises 17–23 in Chapter Two before singing these examples. If needed, draw a box around each beat to help train your eye to see the relationship between the beat and the rhythm. Conduct all exercises!

60. *Allegro con spirito*

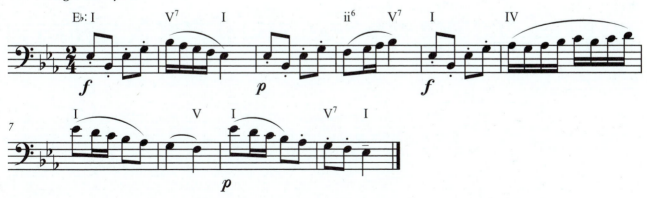

 The next five melodies introduce rests, especially to show phrasing and to indicate places to breathe.

61. *Rhythmic*

62. *Doloroso*

63. *Lento*

64. *Largetto*

65. *Allegretto*

66. *Larghetto*

Chorale: "In allen meinen Taten"

The next thirteen melodies introduce compound meter ($\frac{6}{8}$). In compound meters, a dotted rhythmic value (dotted quarter, dotted eighth, or dotted sixteenth, etc.) gets the beat, and each beat divides into three parts. Review the basic divisions with rhythm exercises 39–52 in Chapter Two before singing these melodies. Make sure you understand the relationship between the beat and its divisions. Mark your music with boxes if needed.

67. *Andantino*

68. *Andantino*

69. *Allegretto*

70. *Allegretto*

71. *Allegro*

72. *Allegro*

73. *Moderato*

74. *Adagietto*

75. *Animato*

▨ ▨ ▨ The next four melodies introduce the dotted eighth-sixteenth rhythm in §time. See rhythm exercises 50–52 in Chapter Two.

76. *Con spirito*

77. *Con anima*

78. *Con anima*

79. *Andante*

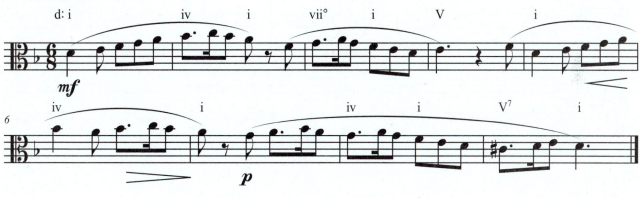

The next four melodies are in the compound meters $\frac{9}{8}$ and $\frac{12}{8}$. For additional drills in compound meters, see Chapter Two beginning with exercise 85.

80. *Larghetto*

81. *Swaying*

82. *Allegretto*

83. *Moderato*

84. *Andante cantabile*

85. *Allegro*

86. *Andantino* **(in one)**

87. *Lentement*   Handel: *Water Music* **(transposed)**

The next five melodies begin with the 5th of the tonic triad.

88. *Allegro*

89. *Larghetto*

90. *Playful*

91. *Andante pastorale*

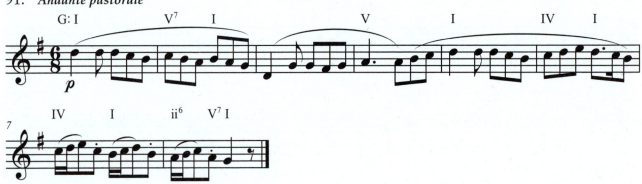

92. *Espressivo*

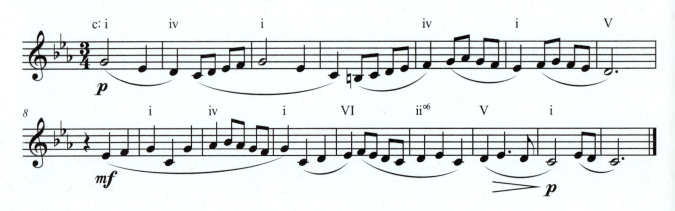

The next five melodies begin with the 3rd of the tonic triad.

93. *Moderato*

94. *Allegro*

95. *With spirit*   **Appalachia, USA**

96. *Andantino*

97. *Allegro con spirito*

98. *Andante*

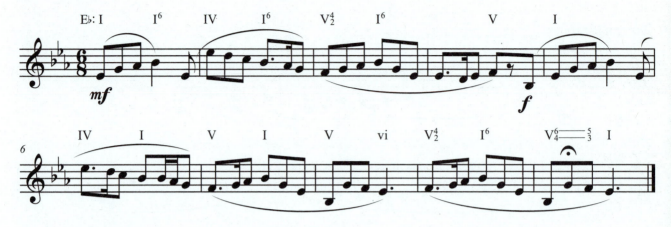

99. *Frisch und munter*

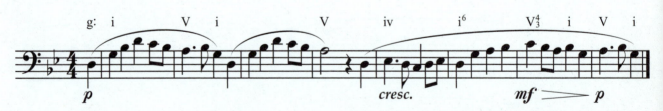

▨ ▨ ▨   The next five melodies begin with upbeats. For additional drills with upbeats, see rhythm exercises 53–56 in Chapter Two.

100. *Allegro moderato*

101. *Andantino*

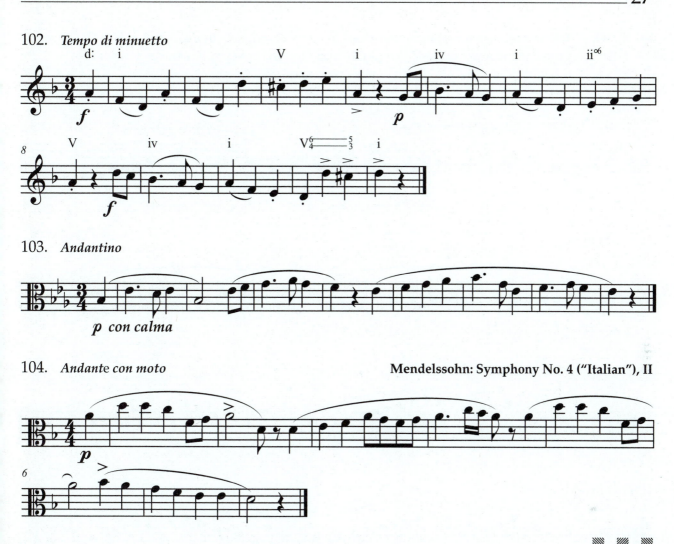

102. *Tempo di minuetto*

103. *Andantino*

104. *Andante con moto* **Mendelssohn: Symphony No. 4 ("Italian"), II**

The + in measure 6 indicates an augmented chord. In the accompaniment, the fifth of the V chord, B♭, is raised to B♮.

105. *Langsam* **Schubert: Wiegenlied**

The next thirteen melodies contain skips in the IV chord, in both major and minor. The IV serves a pre-dominant function and is typically major in a major key and minor in a minor key.

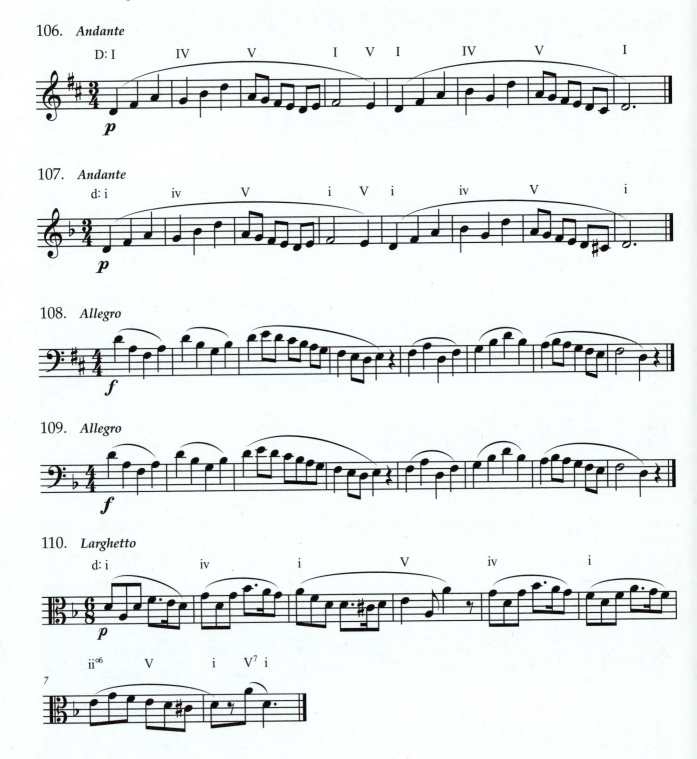

111. *Larghetto*

112. *Allegro*

113. *Allegro*

114. *Adagio*   **Weber: Overture to *Der Freischütz***

115. *Moderate*

116. *Moderato*

117. *Andante con moto*

118. *Allegro*

119. *Valse*

120. *Tempo di menuetto*

121. *Con moto*

122. *Langsam*

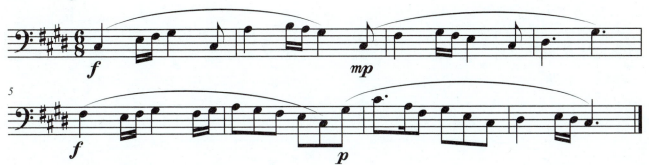

123. *Andante con moto*

124. *Larghetto*

The next nine melodies include skips of the V chord, in both major and minor. The V chord serves a dominant function, and is most often a major chord in a minor key. Which scale step is altered to create the major V chord in the minor mode?

125. *Vif et léger*

132. *Minuetto*

133. *Menuetto*

Haydn: String Quartet in G, Op. 17, No. 5, II

134. *Largo*

135. *Mässig*

E: I   IV   I   V   I   IV   V⁷   I

136. *Avec mouvement*

137. *Allegretto*   **Mozart:** *Così fan tutte*, **Act II, No. 26**

138. *Allegro giocoso*

139. *Allegro moderato*

140. *Risoluto*

141. *Stately*

142. *Moderato*

143. *Animato*

144. *Ben ritmico*

145. *Adagietto*

146. *Not too quickly*

147. *Asseg lent*

The next ten melodies contain skips in the ii chord, in both major and minor. The ii chord is the most common pre-dominant chord in classical tonal music and is generally voiced in first inversion (ii^6). It is minor in a major key, and diminished in a minor key.

148. *Allegro*   **Beethoven: Violin Concerto, I**

149. *Molto allegro*   **Haydn: String Quartet in G, Op. 76, No. 1, movement I**

150. *Moderato*

151. *Moderato*

157. *Deliberatamente*

158. *Cantabile*

159. *Valse*

The next ten melodies introduce skips in the V^7 chord, in both major and minor.

160. *Andante*

166. *Slowly*

167. *Slowly*

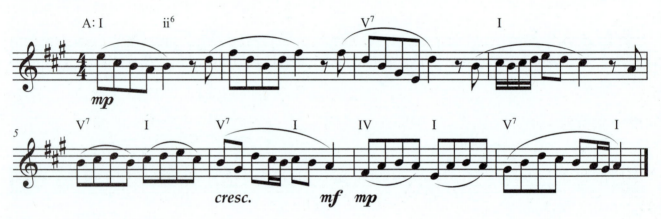

168. *Andantino*   **Mozart:** *Magic Flute, I.7*

169. *Allegretto*   **Mozart: Symphony No. 39, III**

The next seven melodies include skips of the vii° chord, in major and minor. The vii chord is typically diminished in both major and minor keys, has a dominant function, and is frequently found in first inversion. Note that the three notes of the vii° chord are the same as the upper three notes of the V^7 chord. V^7 can also be used to harmonize the notes of the vii° triad, and is the more typical harmonization. Because of the typically restricted uses of the vii°⁶ chord—often passing between I and I^6—all seven subsequent melodies are harmonized.

170. *Moderato*

171. *Moderato*

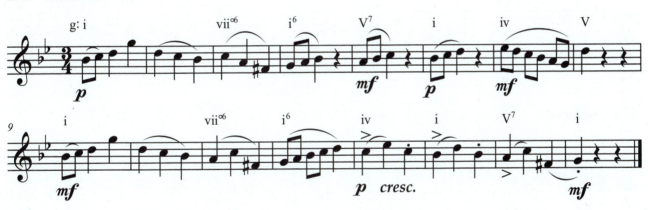

172. *Swaying*

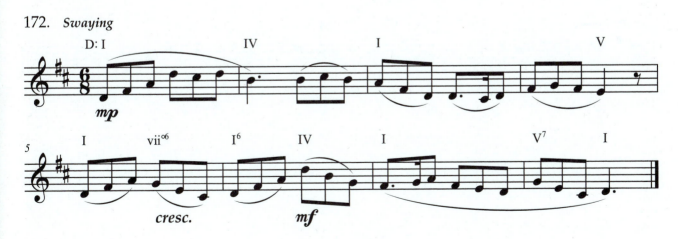

173. *Swaying*

174. *Allegro*

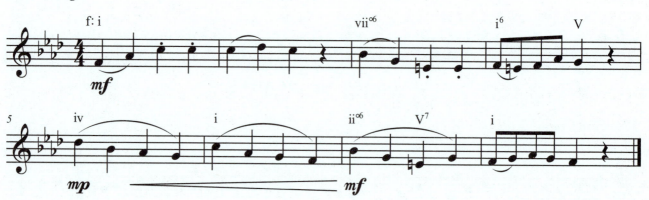

175. *Cheerful*

176. *Vivace*   **Sweden**

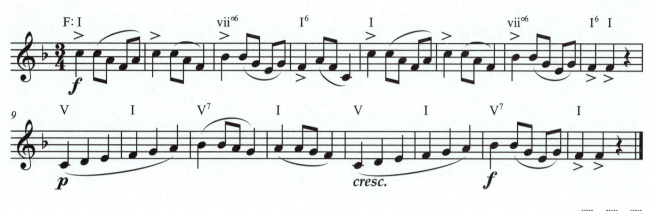

The next eight melodies contain skips in the vi chord, in both major and minor. The vi chord, minor in major keys and major in minor keys, frequently precedes pre-dominant chords or occurs after the dominant chord in a deceptive cadence.

177. *Animato*

178. *Animato*

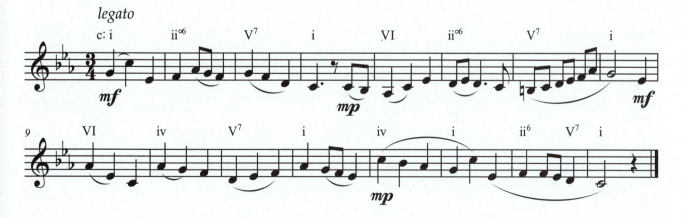

179. *Andante*

180. *Andante*

181. *Brisk*

182. *Brisk*

183. *Moderato*

184. *Marziale*

MELODIES ▨ **SECTION II**

To be used with Section II of all other chapters

These melodies introduce the tenor clef, more comp-plex rhythms, syncopation, and diatonic skips in a variety of contexts, and offer practice singing various intervals. Harmonically, this section introduces sim-ple modulations, secondary dominants, arpeggiation of diatonic harmonies, and altered chords, namely Neapolitan and augmented sixth chords. This section also introduces modal melodies, and the vocal range is extended.

▨ ▨ ▨   The following eight melodies review material from Chapter One, Section I, including arpeggiat-ions of the I, ii, IV, V, V^7 and vii° chords.

185. *Moderato*

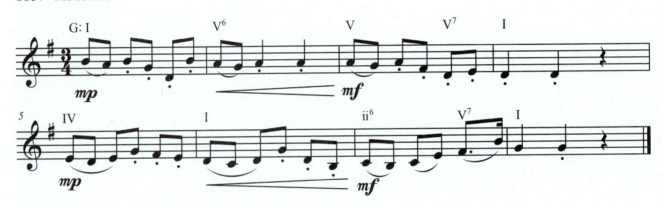

186. *Pastorale*

187. *Cheerfully*

188. *Allegretto*

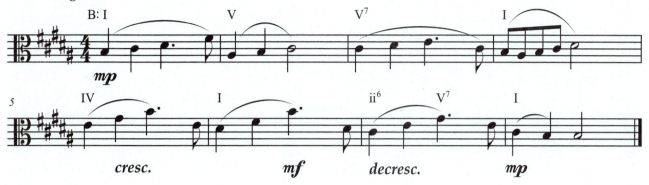

189. *Amabile*

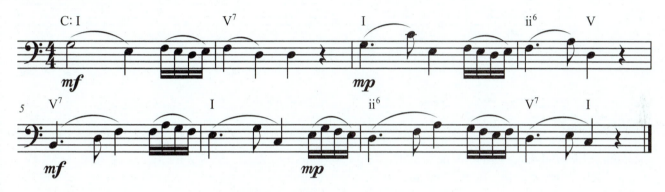

190. *Barcarolle*

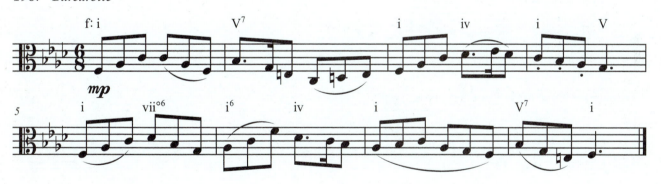

191. *Andante*

192. *Andante*   **Mozart:** *Così fan tutte*, **Act I, No. 10, adapted**

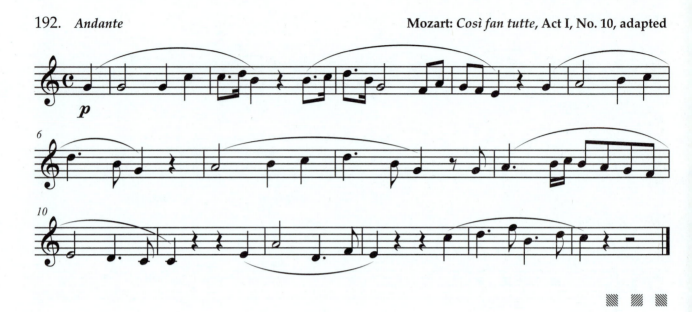

Tenor Clef

Like the alto clef, the tenor clef can be visualized in relation to the grand staff, but the five lines of the tenor clef are not right in the middle of the grand staff. In addition to middle C (indicated with the center of the clef) the staff lines represent the top three lines of the bass clef, and the bottom line of the treble.

Compare the same pitches notated in four clefs:

For the tenor clef, the G above middle C is the first ledger line, middle C is the fourth line, and the second line is F below middle C.

Think of the way you already recognize the same pitches notated in treble and bass clefs.

Refocusing familiar reference points will help you see the way tenor clef renotates familiar pitches.

As with the alto clef, a good way to practice your facility with the tenor clef is to play melodies on the piano. This reinforces the correct placement of the notes of these clefs.

The next eight melodies are written in the tenor clef and are primarily scalar for ease of reading. Note that the first exercise begins on the fourth degree of the scale.

193. *Moderato*

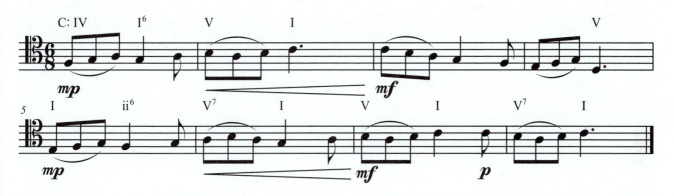

194. *Grave*

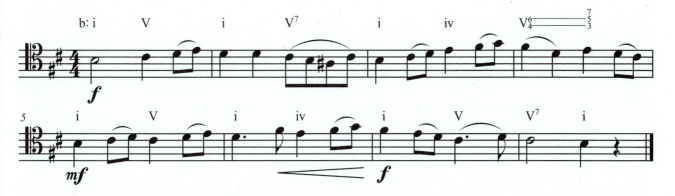

195. *Cheerfully*

196. *Amabile*

197. *Playful*

198. *Cheerfully*

199. *Martial*

200. *Adagio*

Fauré: *Requiem*, **Pie Jesu**

p dolce

201. **Larghetto**

p

9

f

poco rit.

p

202. **Allegro**

mp

cresc.

mf

6

f

p

ff

203. **Andantino**

A♭: I   V⁷   I   D♭: I   V⁷   I

p

mf

A♭: V   V⁷   I   V   V⁷   I   V   I

9

f

p

The next six melodies introduce $\frac{3}{8}$ and $\frac{6}{4}$ time. Depending on the tempo, $\frac{3}{8}$ time may be conducted in 1 or in 3; $\frac{6}{4}$ is conducted in 2. See also rhythm exercises 25, 27, 28, 57, 58, 81, and 82 in Chapter Two.

204. *Allegro con spirito*

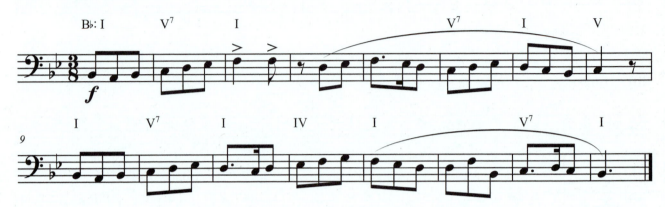

In tonal music progressions, the tendency is for the dominant to lead to the tonic, and that is where it goes in the vast majority of cases. On occasion, however, the IV chord will follow the dominant. This occurs when the composer wants to arrest the motion of the progression, or on occasions when the succession of dominant to predominant has the affect of a deceptive motion. Note the V–IV sequence of chords in mm. 5–6 of the next example, and in the occasional subsequent examples in the book.

205. *Andante cantabile*

206. *Vivo*

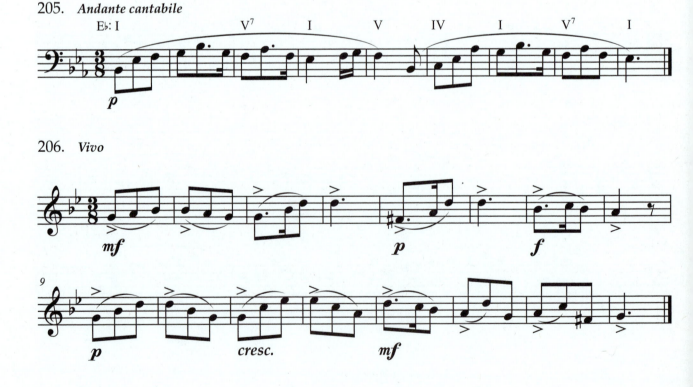

207. *Cantabile*

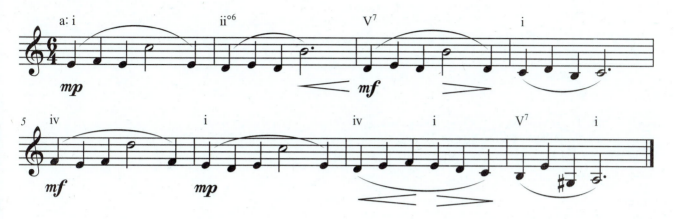

208. *Pastorale*

209. *Piacevole*

210. *Doux et expressif*

211. *Larghetto*

212. *Andante con moto*

Eighth note triplets are introduced in the next two exercises. See rhythm exercises beginning with exercise 108 in Chapter Two for additional practice in triplets.

213. *Bewegt*

214. *Andante con moto*

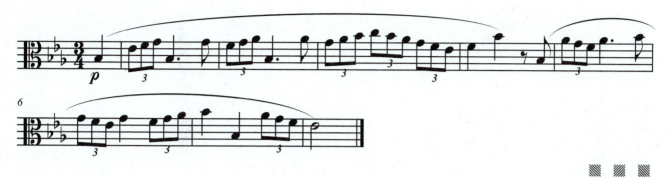

215. *Andante*

The next four melodies practice the interval of a perfect fifth.

216. *Allegretto*

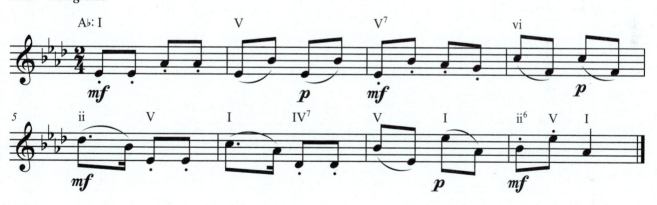

217. *Lento*

218. *March-like*

219. *Lustig*

 Skips of all diatonic intervals up to an octave are included from this point on.

220. *Andante con moto*

221. *Lentement*

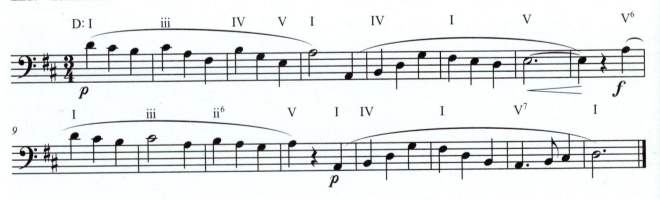

222. *Langsam*

Ties are included in many of the melodies from this point on. See rhythm exercises beginning at exercise 114 in Chapter Two for additional practice with ties.

223. *Allegretto*

224. *Vivace*

225. *Alla marcia*

The next six melodies begin with upbeats ♪ or ♫. See rhythm exercises 117–121 in Chapter Two for additional practice with pickups.

226. *Allegro marziale*

227. *Andante pastorale*

228. *Allegro*

229. *Con moto*

230. *Allegro*

231. *Gaio*

Syncopations are introduced in the next six melodies. See rhythm exercises 122–141 in Chapter Two for additional practice in syncopation.

232. *Jaunty*

233. *Sustained*

234. *Gaio*

235. *Largo*

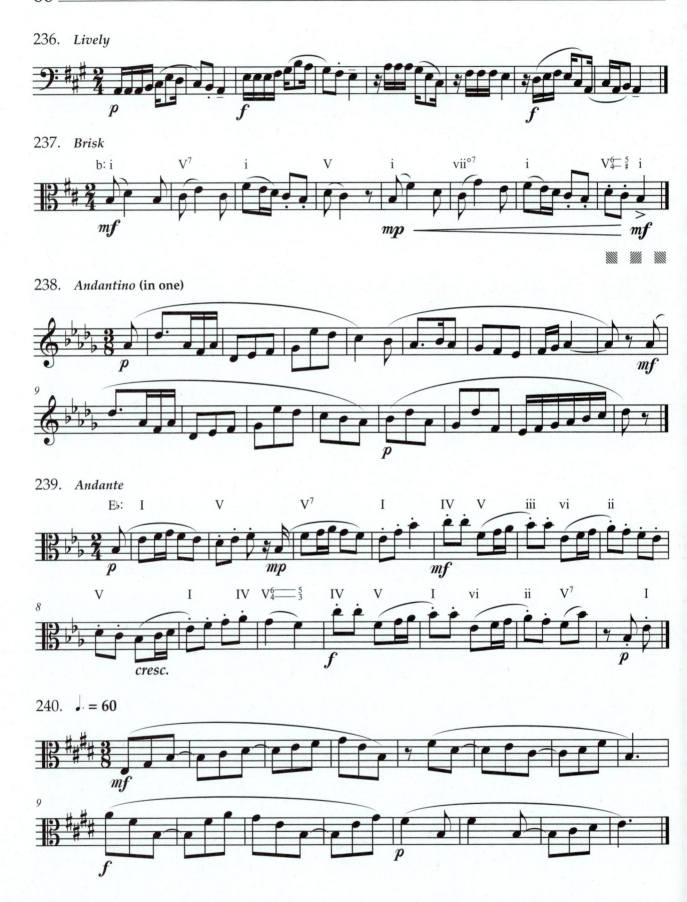

241. *Allegretto*

242. *Maestoso*   Mozart: *Così fan tutte*, **Act I, No. 8, transposed**

243. *Tempo di polaca*   Mussorgsky: *Boris Gudonov*, **Act III**

 The next four exercises practice intervals of a sixth.

244. *Gemütlich*

245. *Andantino grazioso*

246. *Adagio*

247. *Moderato*

Accidentals in tonal music are sometimes diatonic (the raised sixth and seventh degrees in minor, for example), sometimes ornamental, and sometimes suggest other keys. You should discern the function of accidentals, that is, whether they are embellishments of a note in the tonic scale or whether they serve to tonicize a key other than the tonic. The next four melodies contain chromatic neighbor tones, all of which function within the key and all of which should be harmonized diatonically. When non-key tones are ornamental, you should strive to hear them in relation to notes within the key. See duets exercises 57–59 in Chapter Three.

248. *Andante*

249. *Andante*

250. *Andantino piacevole*

251. *Moderato*

252. *Mässig und zart*

253. *Moderato con moto*

254. *Cheerful*

▨ ▨ ▨   The next four melodies, in the minor mode, move through the relative major. Before singing, find the point where that motion begins.

255. *Allegro*

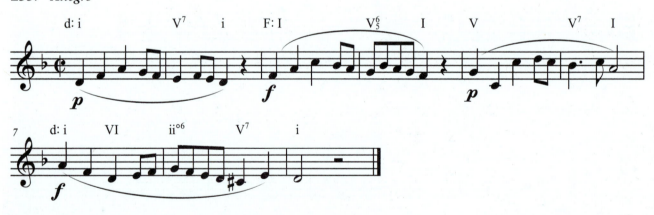

256. *Allegro moderato*

257. *Larghetto*

258. *Andantino*

259. *Andante*

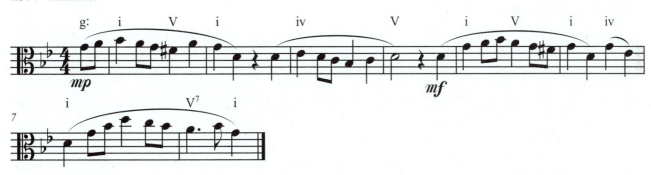

260. *Allegro moderato*

The next five melodies include chromatic passing notes. See duets exercises 63–66 in Chapter Three.

261. *Moderato*

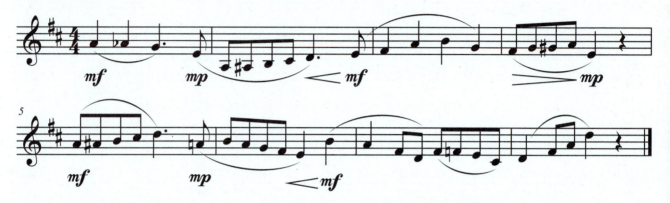

262. *Moderato con moto*

263. *Andante con moto*

264. *Allegro non troppo*

265. *Allegro con spirito*

Haydn: *Lord Nelson Mass,* **Credo**

266. *Maestoso*

267. *Animé*

268. *Lento*

269. *Slowly*

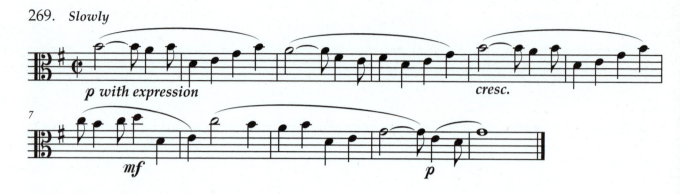

270. *Andante con moto*

▨ ▨ ▨ The next four melodies, in the major mode, move through the dominant.

271. *Allegretto grazioso*

272. *Allegro assai*

273. *Allegretto*

274. *Ländler*

The next four melodies tonicize the key of the dominant.

275. *Andantino*   Mozart: *Magic Flute*, **I.7**

276. *Lieblich*   Schubert: *Heidenröslein* (transposed)

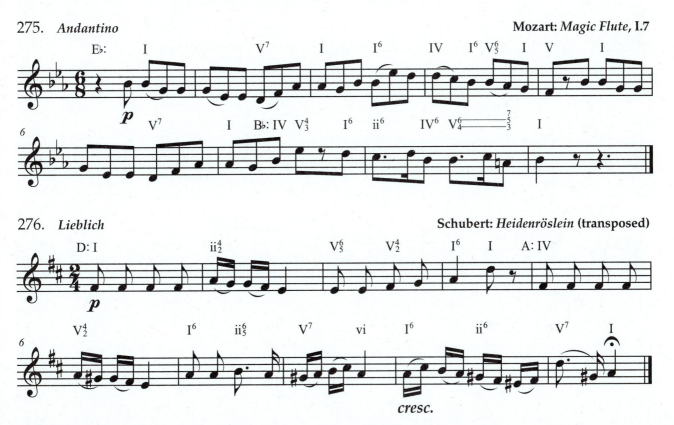

Find and mark the point in the next two melodies where the dominant key is tonicized. This will assist in hearing the direction of the melody as well as aid intonation.

277. *Trio*   **Haydn: Symphony No. 104, III**

278. *Lebendig*   **Schumann:** *Dichterliebe*, **15 (transposed)**

 The next three melodies move to or through the key of the subdominant.

279. *Lively*

Find and mark in the next example the point where the melody is harmonized in the key of the subdominant.

280.   *Allegro Moderato*   **Mussorgsky**, *Boris Gudonov*, **Act IV**

Find and mark the points in the next melody where the subdominant key is tonicized and the tonic key returns.

281.   *Moderato*

The next ten melodies include secondary dominants. Be aware of which accidentals suggest secondary dominants and which are ornamental and should be harmonized (and heard) diatonically. In the next melody, for example, all of the accidentals are ornamental, except for the B♮ in measure 5, which suggests a secondary dominant of V. Tonicizations in duets begin in exercise 63 of Chapter Three.

282. *Fliessend*

283. *Moderato*

284. *Andante*

285. *Valse* **(in one)**

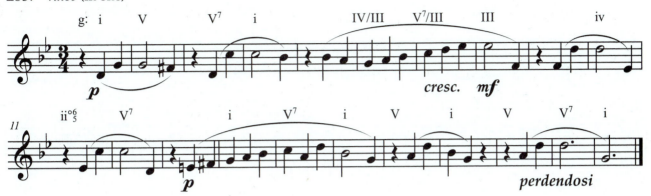

286. *Moderato*

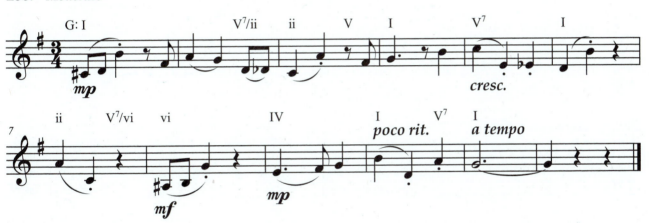

287. *Lively*

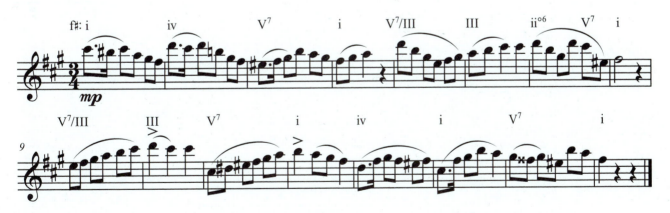

288. *Andantino*

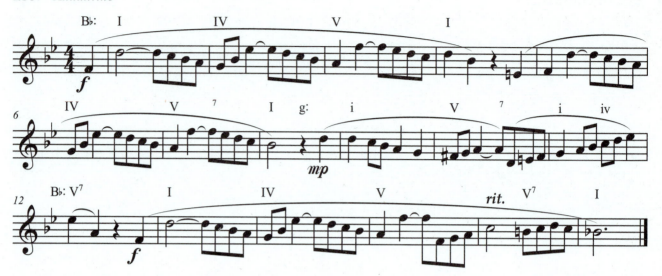

Find and mark in the next three melodies secondary dominants and/or temporary changes of key.

289. *Allegro e ben marcato*

290. *Allegro moderato*

D.C. al Fine

12

p subito

291. *Modéré*

p   *pp*   *mf*

6

p

▨ ▨ ▨   The next four melodies practice intervals of a tritone (the general term for augmented fourths and diminished fifths). As in all cases, an awarness of the harmonic context of these intervals will allow you to better hear them and sing better in tune. The tritone found in the first measure of the next two exercises comprises the third and seventh of the V^7 chord. Playing the chord will make hearing and singing the interval much easier.

292. *Cheerfully*

293. *Slow and somber*

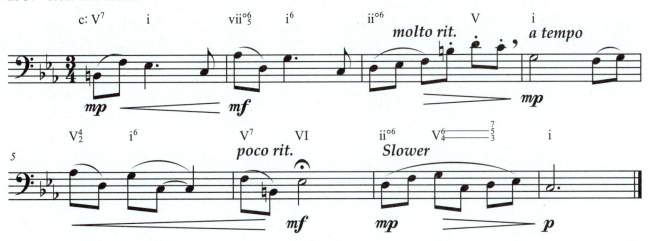

294. *Con moto*

295. *Flowing*   **"Santa Lucia" (Italy)**

296. *Etwas gedehnt*

The next four melodies treat the Neapolitan (lowered supertonic) chord. In the Neapolitan, which functions as a pre-dominant chord, the root is lowered one-half step. When the root is lowered one-half step in the minor key, the result is a major chord. Since the Neapolitan is a major chord in both major and minor keys, both the root and the fifth of the ii chord must be lowered by one half step in major keys. The Neapolitan is most frequently found in first inversion, forming a Neapolitan sixth (N^6). In the following three melodies, the N^6 chord is arpeggiated to better illustrate the components of the chord. In the subsequent melody, from the literature, the melody in measure 6 is accompanied by a Neapolitan sixth chord. Where the N^6 is found below, you will want to accompany the melody with block chords in first inversion.

297. *Moderato*

298. *Allegro commodo*

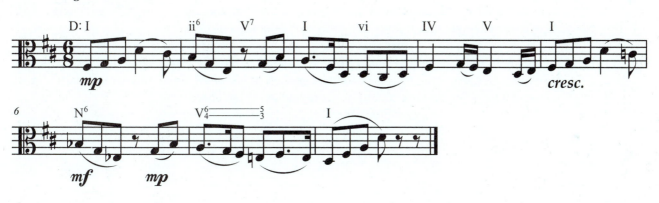

299. *Zart*

300. *Mässig*   Schubert: *Die Schöne Mullerin*, **No. 19 (transposed)**

*Play a bass note "e" below the V chord.

Augmented sixth chords function as pre-dominants. These chords are derived from characteristic chromatically-inflected voice leading to the dominant. Each variant of the augmented sixth chord includes a note that is a semitone above (♭6) and a semitone below (♯4) the fifth scale degree, creating, in effect, *two* leading tones to the dominant. These two notes spell the interval of an augmented sixth when found with the raised fourth degree of the scale voiced above the sixth degree of the minor scale. (In the major mode, both notes of the A⁶ interval are chromatic; in the minor mode, only the ♯4 is a chromatic tone.)

There are three main types of augmented sixth chords: the Italian sixth (It⁶): minor scale degrees 6, 1, and raised 4; the German sixth (Gr⁶): minor scale degrees 6, 1, 3, and raised 4; and the French sixth (Fr⁶): minor scale degrees 6, 1, 2, and raised 4. Note that all three of these variants include the three scale degrees of the It⁶ form. (Other terminologies to identify augmented sixth chords—for example, Gr⁶₅, It⁶, and Fr⁴₃—are also commonly used.)

The next six melodies treat augmented sixth chords. Augmented sixth chords are spelled the same way in both major and minor keys. The chord is usually found accompanying melodies. However, the next three melodies contain arpeggiations of all three augmented sixth chords, which will help familiarize you with the components of the chord.

301. *Relaxed*

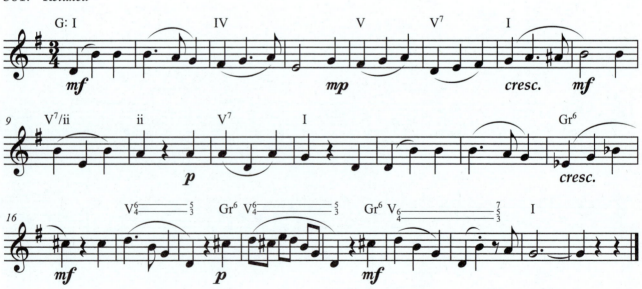

302. *Gioviale*

303. *Allegretto*

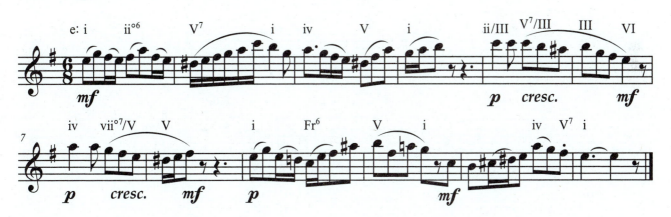

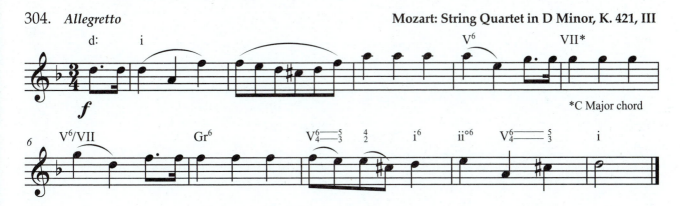

The next three melodies have notes that are accompanied by augmented sixth chords. Play block chords to accompany those measures.

304. *Allegretto*

Mozart: String Quartet in D Minor, K. 421, III

*C Major chord

305. *Allegro ma non troppo*   **Schubert: String Quartet in A Minor, I**

306. *Waltz tempo*

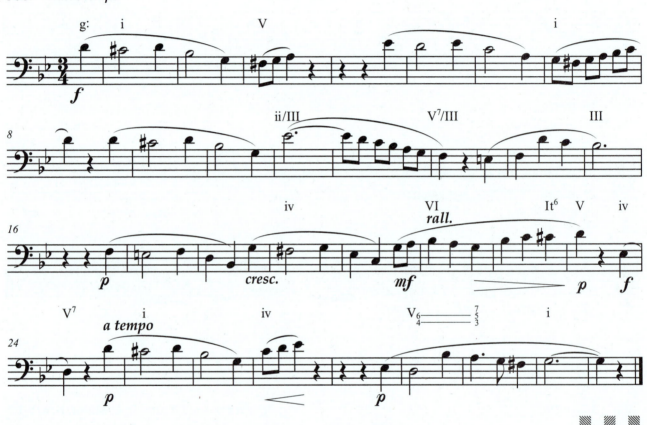

Section II concludes with a group of melodies based on these four modes. Duets using these modes are found beginning in exercise 72 in Chapter Three.

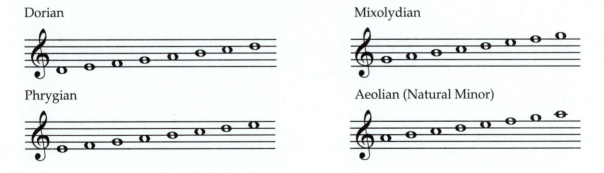

Listen to the characteristic aspects of the Dorian mode in the next four examples. These include the minor i and v chords, along with the major IV and VII chords.

307. *Andante* **(Dorian)**

308. *Andante con moto* **(transposed Dorian)**

309. *Dance* **(transposed Dorian)**

310. *Melancholy* **(transposed Dorian)**

311.   *Lento* **(Phrygian)**

Here, the suggested harmonization includes the major I, minor v, and major ♭VII chords.

312.   *Brightly* **(transposed Mixolydian)**

313.   *Mässig* **(Mixolydian)**

314.   *Allegro ma non troppo* **(Mixolydian)**

315. *Vivement* **(transposed Mixolydian)**

316. *Moving forward* **(Aeolian)**

317. *Lento* **(Aeolian)**

318. *Andante sostenuto* **(transposed Aeolian)**

MELODIES ▧ *SECTION III*

To be used with Section III of all other chapters

Chromatic alterations are used with increasing frequency in melodies of this section. Some indicate modulation; some are factors in secondary dominant harmonies; others are melodic embellishments. Within these melodies there is an increasing diversity of rhythms, intervals, phrase structures, and musical styles.

The material of Section III readily can be correlated with the study of chromatic harmony.

The following eight melodies review material from Chapter One, Section II, and at a similar level of difficulty. These melodies contain syncopation, major and minor sixths, phrases in major and its relative minor, chromatic neighbor and chromatic passing tones, secondary dominants, and melodies accompanied by Neapolitan 6 and augmented sixth chords.

▧ ▧ ▧   The following two melodies contain syncopations.

319. *Presto*   Haydn: Symphony No. 80, IV

320. *Allegro ma non troppo*   Dvořák: String Quartet, Op. 96, I

▧ ▧ ▧

The following melody practices major sixth and minor sixth intervals.

321. *Allegro vivace*   **Mozart: Symphony No. 41 ("Jupiter"), I**

The following melody moves through the relative major and contains an augmented sixth chord in the accompaniment in m. 11.

322. *Barcarolle*

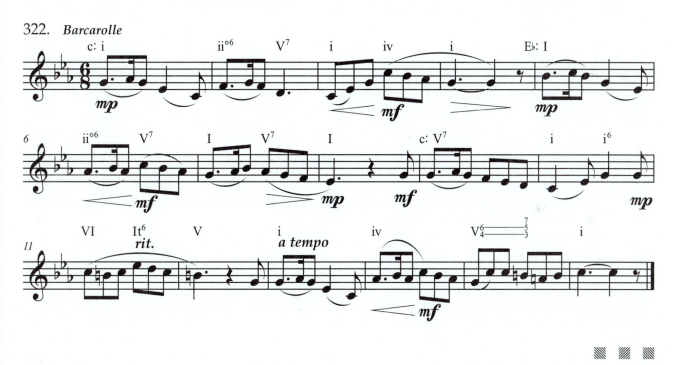

The following three melodies contain chromatic neighbor and/or chromatic passing tones.

323. *Moderato*   **Wagner:** *Tannhäuser*, **Act III**

324. *Cheerful*

325. *Allegro vivace e con brio*   **Beethoven: Symphony No. 8, I**

The following melody contains a passage accompanied by a secondary dominant. Identify and mark the tonicization.

326. *Allegro non troppo*   **Brahms: Symphony No. 1, IV**

Skips larger than one octave are found in the next four melodies.

327. *Allegro*

328. *Allegro moderato*

329. *Andante con moto*

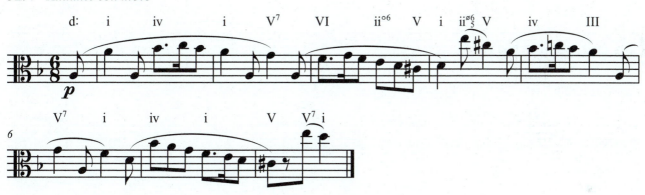

See rhythm exercises 167–172 in Chapter Two for additional practice in quarter note triplets.

330. *Allegro deciso*

331. *Scherzando*

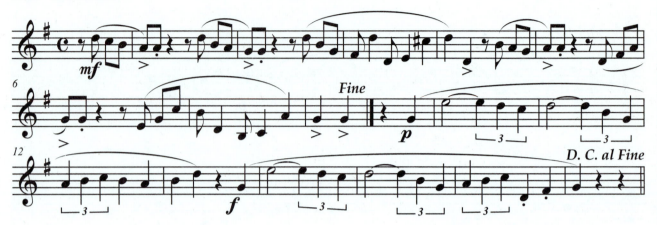

332. *Ballad*

333. *Allegro con brio*

The following five melodies introduce thirty-second notes and dotted sixteenth-thirty second note rhythms.

334. *Andante con moto*   **Schubert: Symphony No. 5, II**

335. *Mit Kraft*

The next three melodies add sixteenth-note triplets. See exercises 178, 184, and 185 in Chapter Two to practice sixteenth-note triplets.

336. *Con moto*   **Hungary**

337. *Andante ed espressivo*

338. *Andante con moto*

Beethoven: Symphony No. 5, II

339. *Largo e mesto*

340. *Lively*

341. *Grazioso*

342. *Swaying*

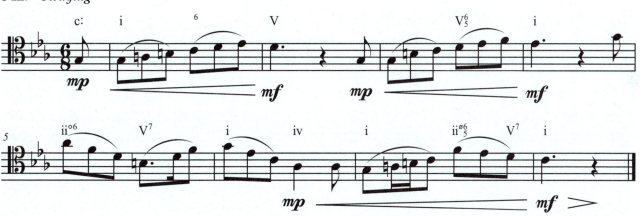

343. *Anima*

344. *Dolorous*

345. *Larghetto*

▨ ▨ ▨ The next three melodies practice intervals of a sixth.

346. *Moderato*

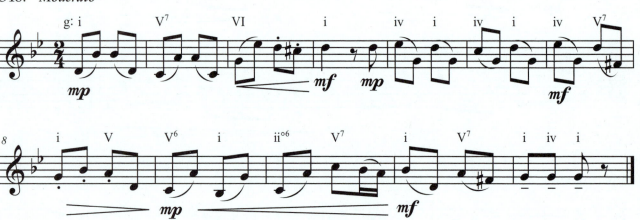

347. *Dolce*

348. *Andante*

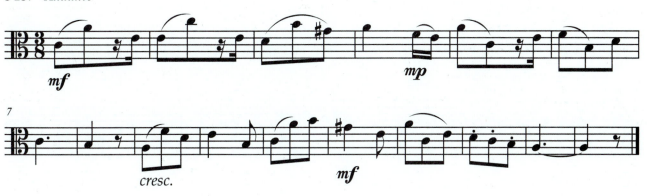

349. *Allegro*   **Berlioz: *Roman Carnival Overture***

Skips to chromatic notes are introduced in the next six melodies. Such skips often create awkward intervals that are challenging to hear and sing. Relating the chromatic notes to those in the key will help you to hear and sing the pitches. Sometimes chromatic tones are ornamental; they do not suggest a different key. Sometimes, they indicate a change of key. Knowing the key of every passage will help you hear and sing the chromatic notes correctly.

There are many chromatic notes in the following melody. The first, in m. 2, is clearly ornamental. The G♯ in m. 4 suggests a tonicization of the dominant chord. It will help you to hear it that way. While the remaining accidentals could be harmonized in more complicated ways, it is easiest to hear them as ornaments to notes of the tonic triad.

350. *Allegro moderato*

In the next example, in measures 4 and 7, hear the A♯ in relationship to the "structural" note, B, to which it is going in mm. 4 and 8.

351.   **Andante molto cantabile ed espressivo**   **Beethoven: Piano Sonata in E Major, Op. 109, III**

352.   *Andante mosso*

353.   *Tempo di valse*

In m. 5 of the following example, the B♮ is not adjacent to a note in the F major scale. The key of C major is tonicized in that passage. The best way to hear the B♮ is as the third of the V chord (a G-major chord) in the key of C. The dominant ninth chord is also introduced in this melody.

354.   *Larghetto*

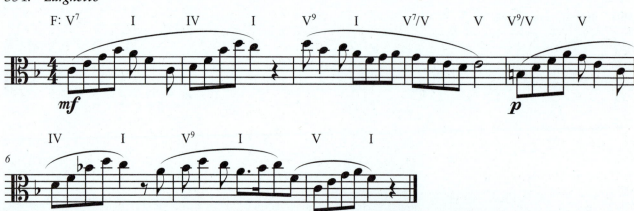

The following example, despite many chromatic notes, can be harmonized entirely in B♭ Major, without any secondary dominants or tonicizations. The chromatic notes are ornaments to pitches within the key. Hear the chromatic notes in relationship to the structural pitches.

355. *Gavotte*

The following twelve melodies introduce minor and major seventh intervals.

356. *Adagio un poco mosso*   **Beethoven: Piano Concerto No. 5 ("Emperor"), II**

357. *Adagio*   **Verdi: Prelude to *La Traviata***

358. *Valse* **(in one)**

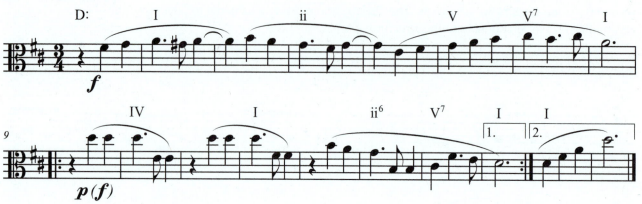

359. *Allegro grazioso*

360. *Andante* **(three-voice cannon)**   **Germany**

361. *Allegro*   **Mozart:** *Così fan tutte,* **Act I, No. 4**

362. *Pas trop lent*

363. *Allegro gioviale*

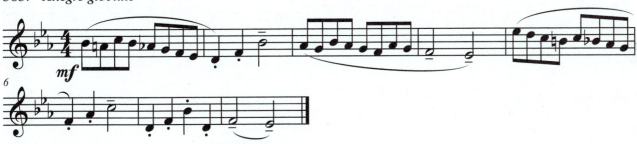

364. *Forthright*

365. *Ländler*

366. *Bewegt*

367. *Allegro lunatico*

368. *Largo e maestoso*

369. *Allegretto*

370. *Andante con moto*

▧ ▨ ▩ The next four melodies move through the subdominant.

371. *Resolute*

372. *Doucement*

373. *Con forza*

374. *Largo*

Dvořák: Symphony No. 9 ("From The New World"), II

375. *Sostenuto ed espressivo*

376. *Allegretto*

377. *Con moto*

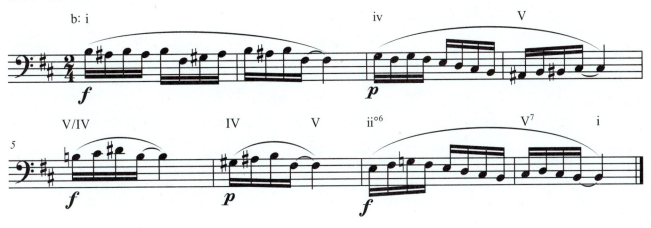

378. *Jaunty*

379. *Marcato*

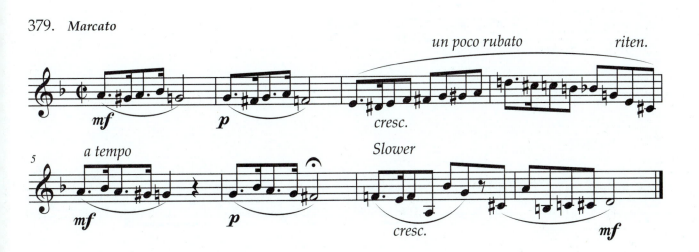

380. *Largo*

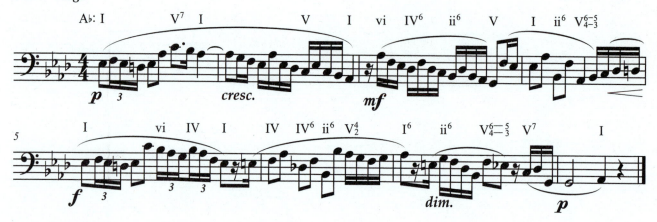

381. *Vivace*

382. *Etwas langsam und zart*

 The next five melodies move through the supertonic.

383. *Adagietto*

384. *Moderato*

385. *Waltzing*

386. *Allegro Moderato* **Mussorgsky:** *Boris Gudonov,* **Act IV**

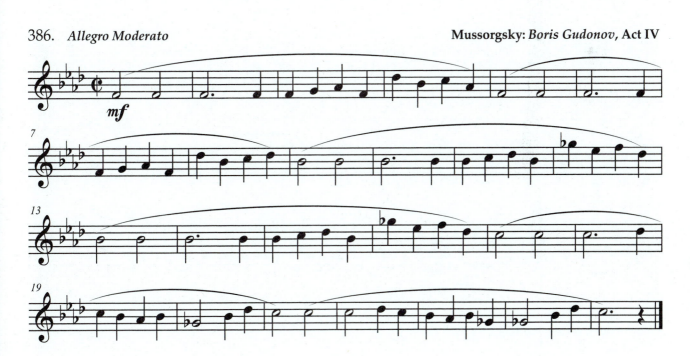

387. *Allegro con spirito*   **Haydn: String Quartet in G, Op. 76, No. 1, I**

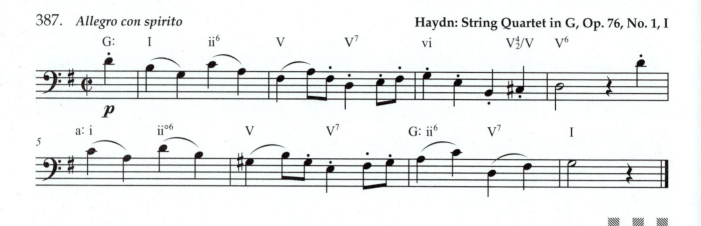

388. *Briskly*

   Secondary dominants and vii°⁷ chords are outlined in the next six melodies.

389. *Energetic*

390. *Andante con moto*

391. *Allegro*

392. *Sehr rasch*

393. *Allegretto*

394. *Brisk*

395. *Innig*

396. *Valse*

397. *Ziemlich bewegt*

398. *Allegretto*

The next four major key melodies move through the submediant.

399. *Gioviale*

400. *Allegro et leggiero*

401. *Amabile*

402. *Tempo marziale*   **Gounod:** *Faust*, **Act IV**

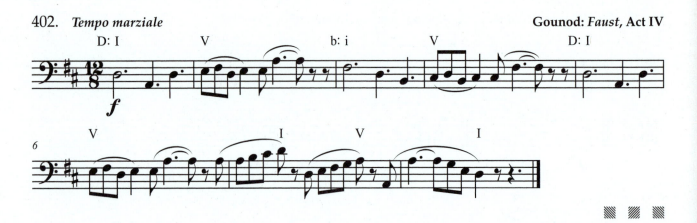

The meters $\frac{5}{8}$ and $\frac{5}{4}$ are introduced in the next six melodies. $\frac{5}{8}$ and $\frac{5}{4}$ can be conducted in 2. See also rhythm exercises 194–203 in Chapter Two for unusual ("odd") meters.

403. *Allegro*

404. *Andantino*

405. *Energetic*

406. *Slowly and simply*

407. *Moderate*

Note the unusual phrase structure in the following melody.

408. *Larghetto*   **Chopin: Piano Sonata No. 1, III**

409. *Lento*

410. **Slow and tender**

411. **Presto**

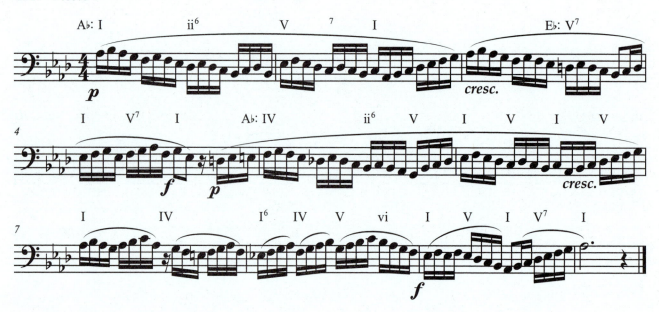

412. **Lilting**

413. *Andantino amabile*

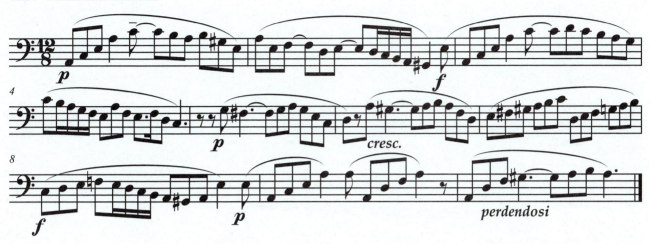

414. *Allegretto*

415. *Animé et très expressif*

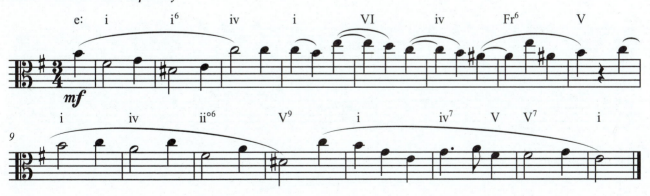

416. *Allegro assai*

417. *Presto alla Tarantella*

418. *Cheerful*

419. *Assez lent*

420. *Andante espressivo*

421. *Rather slowly*

422. *Vif et léger*

423. *Modéré et doucement*

The next five melodies, in the major mode, include the lowered sixth scale degree. The resulting harmonization suggests mode mixture, the borrowing of a chord from the parallel minor. Harmonize the lowered sixth scale degree in the following melodies with iv or VI. Note the Lydian inflection (raised fourth scale degree) in the next exercise, as well as the use of the common tone diminished seventh chord (ct^{o7}). The common tone diminished seventh chord typically leads to a major triad or dominant seventh chord (in the key or a secondary dominant) whose root is the same as one of the notes in the common tone diminished chord. The notes of the common tone diminished seventh chord typically resolve by half or whole step.

424. *Waltz*

425. *Andante*

426. *Andantino*

427. *Tempo di minuetto*

428. *Andante semplice*

429. *Quasi presto*

430. *Allegro giocoso*

431. *Allegretto*

432. *Alla Tarantella*

433. *Allegro gioviale*

434. *Andante ben ritmico*

The minor minor seventh chord figures prominently in the next melody.

435. *Trés calme et document expressif*   **Debussy: "The Girl with the Flaxen Hair"**

The dominant ninth chord, in both major and minor, is outlined in the next four melodies.

436. *Andante*

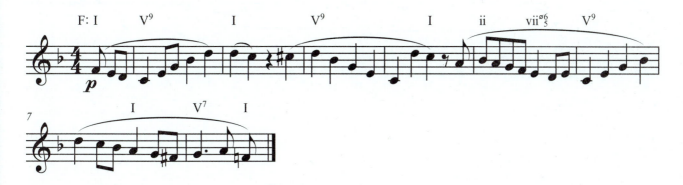

437. *Larghetto*

438. *Andantino*

439. *Adagio ed espressivo*

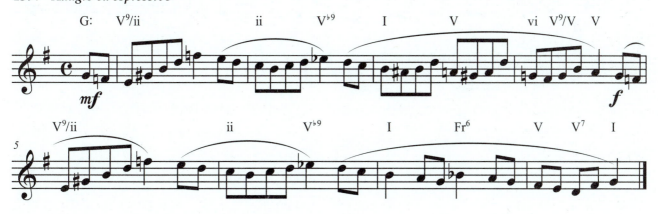

440. *Largo*

441. *Largo*

442. *Vif*

447. *Allegretto*

448. *Il più presto possibile*

449. *Valse*

450. *Alla marcia*

Note the V⁹ chords in mm. 1 and 5 of the next melody.

451.   *Andante e rubato*

452.   *Allegro molto*

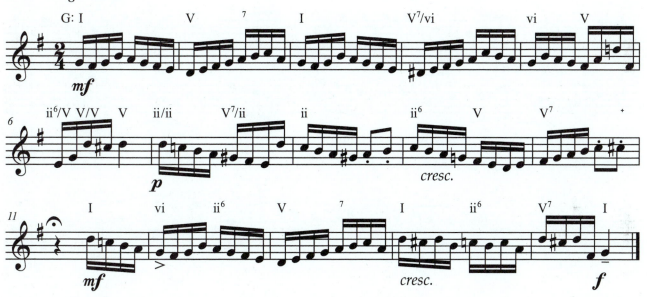

453.   *Allegretto*

454. *Lively*

455. *Vif et gai*

456. *Etwas langsam und zart*

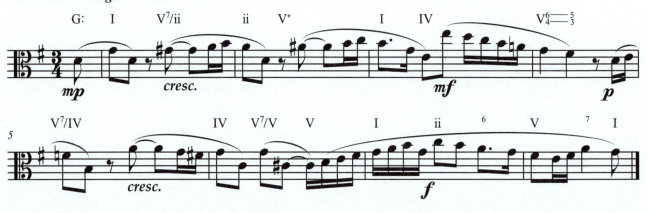

457. *In jig time*

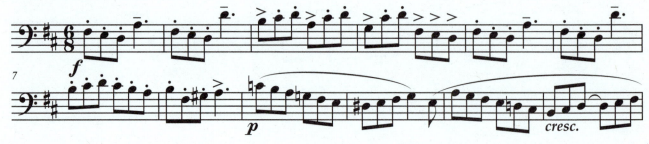

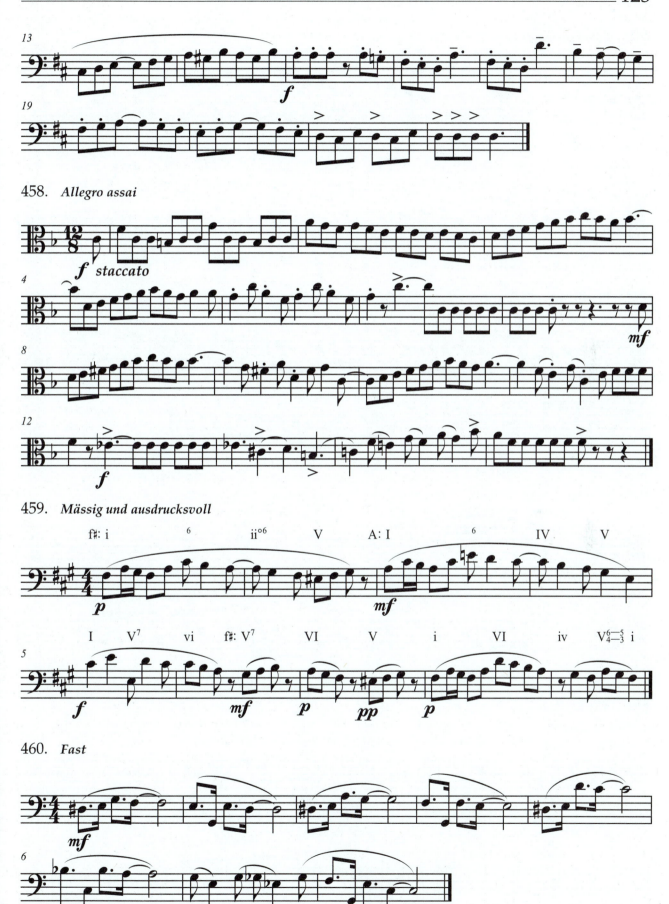

458. *Allegro assai*

459. *Mässig und ausdrucksvoll*

460. *Fast*

461. *Largo con affetto*

462. *Presto*

463. *Lento*

464. *Mit Kraft*

MELODIES *SECTION IV*

To be used with Section IV of all other chapters

The melodies in this section present challenging problems of intonation, rhythm, and phrase structure. Modulation to remote keys, the use of augmented and diminished intervals, a more intensified chromaticism, modal idioms, and complex syncopation offer the advanced student greater challenge.

The concluding melodies of this section introduce tonal twentieth-century idioms.

The first twelve melodies of this section review the major topics of section III including large skips, a wide variety of beat subdivisions, compound meters, syncopation, skips to chromatic notes, leap of the 7th, tonicization of various scale degrees, $\frac{5}{4}$ and $\frac{4}{2}$ time signatures and modal mixture.

465. Allegro

466. Gently

125

467. *Andante con moto*

468. **Largo**

469. **Andante**

470. **Slowly**

471. **Allegro**

472. **Flowing**

473. Slow, like a rag

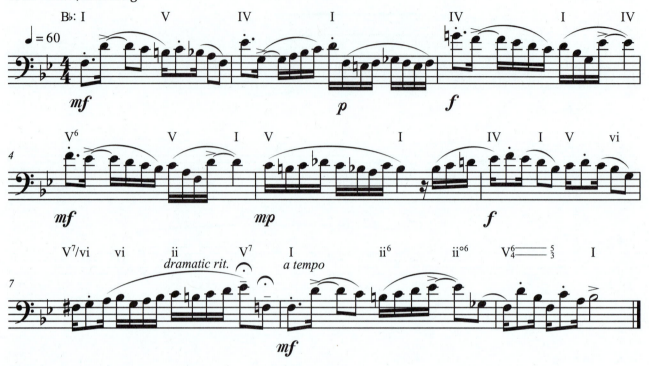

 The next nine melodies are in the alto or tenor clef.

474. *Moderato*

475. *Allegro con grazia* ♩ = 144   **Tchaikovsky: Symphony No. 6, II**

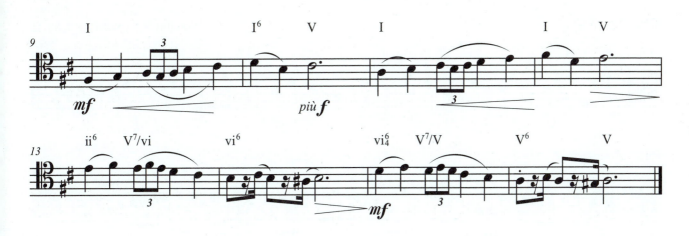

476. *Sostenuto*

477. *Presto*

478. *Allegro deciso*

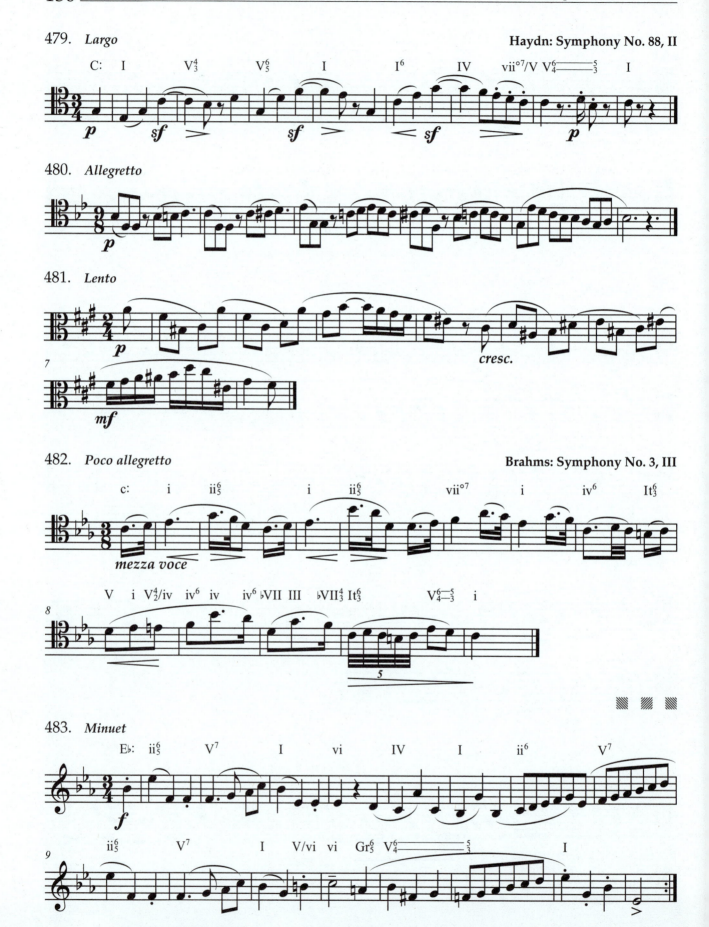

479. *Largo*   **Haydn: Symphony No. 88, II**

480. *Allegretto*

481. *Lento*

482. *Poco allegretto*   **Brahms: Symphony No. 3, III**

483. *Minuet*

484. *Tempo di valzer*

485. *Largo*

Verdi: *Il Trovatore*, **Act II**

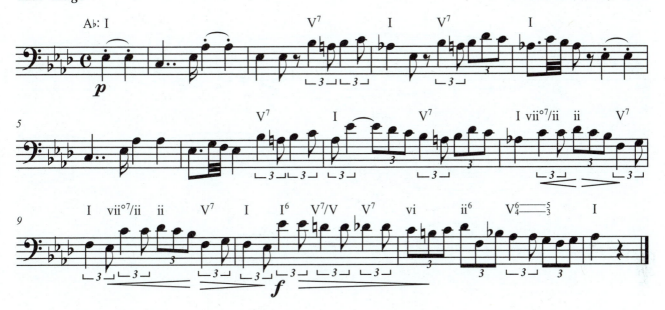

486. *Avec mouvement*

487. *Fliessend*

488. *Andantino*   **Saint-Saëns:** *Samson and Delilah*, **Act II**

489. *Avec mouvement*

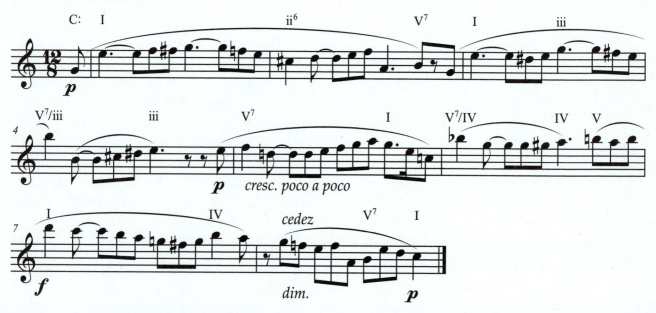

490. **alla Marica**

491. *Con spirito*

492. *Lento*

493. *Con moto*

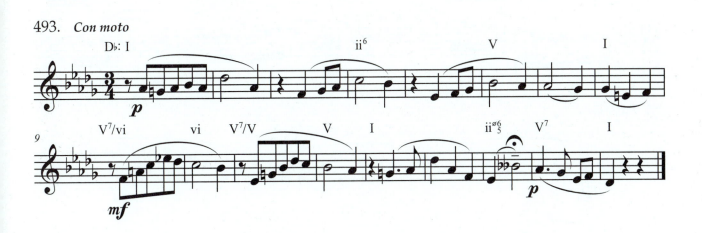

494. *Allegro*   **Weber: Overture to *Oberon***

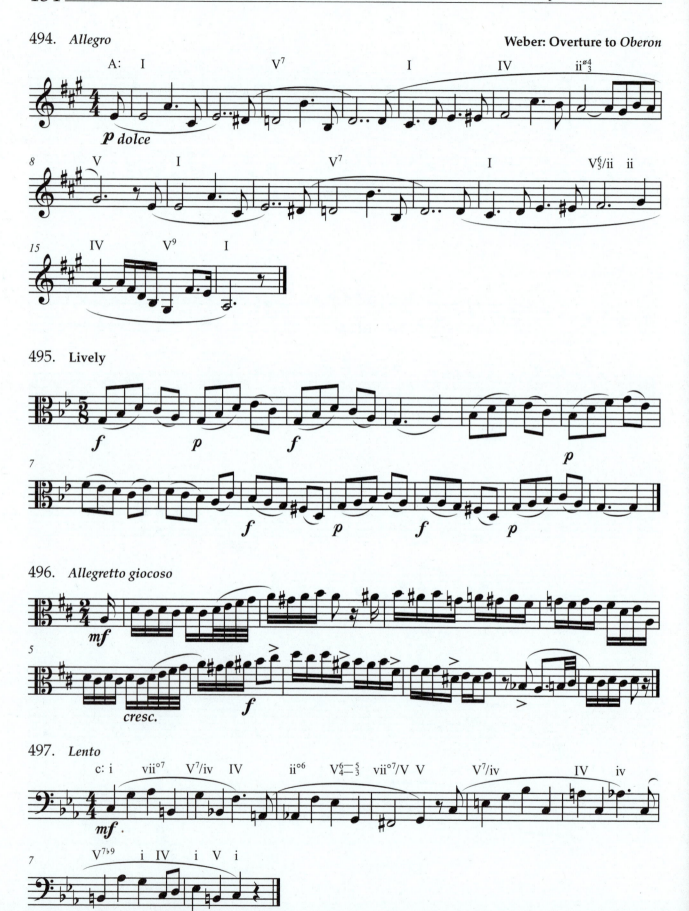

498. *Valse brillante* **(in one)**

Note the unusual harmonic motion to IV, iv and ♭III. Notice how the roman numeral notation identifies both the root and the chord quality.

499. *Sehr langsam und ausdrucksvoll*   **Brahms "Die Mainacht"**

500. *Molto adagio*

501. **Andante misterioso**

502. **Adagio con espressione**

503. **Teneramente**

504. *Sostenuto ed espressivo*

505. *Andantino e leggiero*

506. *Moderato con moto*

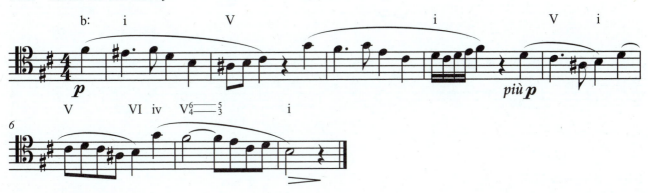

507. *Langsam und ausdrucksvoll*

508. *Allegro energico*

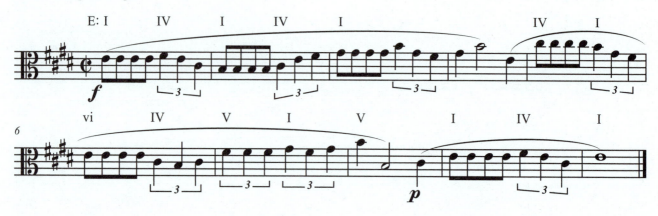

509. *Andante*

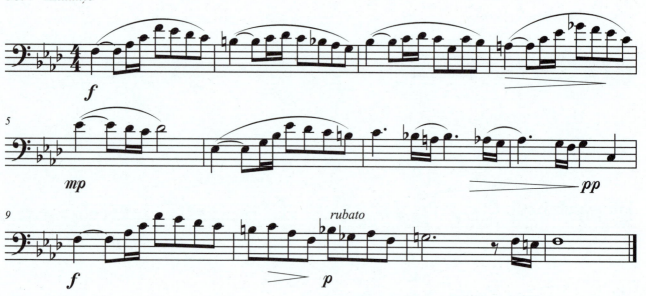

510. *Allegro assai*

511. *Bewegt*

512. *Andante*

513. *Allegro*

514. *Langsam*

515. *Fliessend*

516. *Allegro*

These next two examples from Schumann's *Dichterliebe* explore ♭II and a variety of tonicizations. Note that N⁶ and ♭II⁶ are two different ways of expressing the same sonority: a major triad built on the lowered second degree of the scale. By far the most frequent voicing of this chord has the third in the bass.

517. *Lebhaft*   **Schumann: "Und wüssten's die Blumen"**

518. *Langsam*   **Schumann: "Hör' ich das Liedchen klingen"**

519. *Langsam*

520. *Allegro*

521. *Moderato e pomposo*

522. *Larghetto*

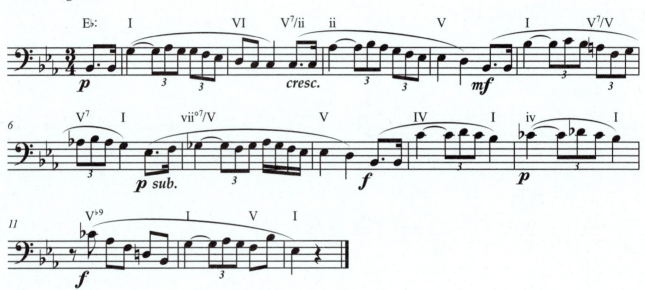

523. *Allegretto*

524. *Allegretto maestoso*

In the next two melodies, notice how the first tonicizes three distinct tonalities, whereas the second includes chromaticism that relates to a single tonic.

525. *Con anima*

526. *Allegretto*

527. *Moderato*

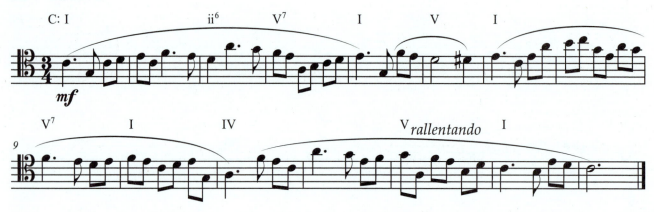

528. *Flowing*

The next two exercises are in ⅞ time. Mixed meters like ⅝ and ⅞ can be conducted by beating the quarter-note or dotted quarter-note beats as they occur, using a standard 2 or 3 conducting pattern. For additional practice, see rhythm exercises 197–200 in Chapter Two.

529. *Spirito*

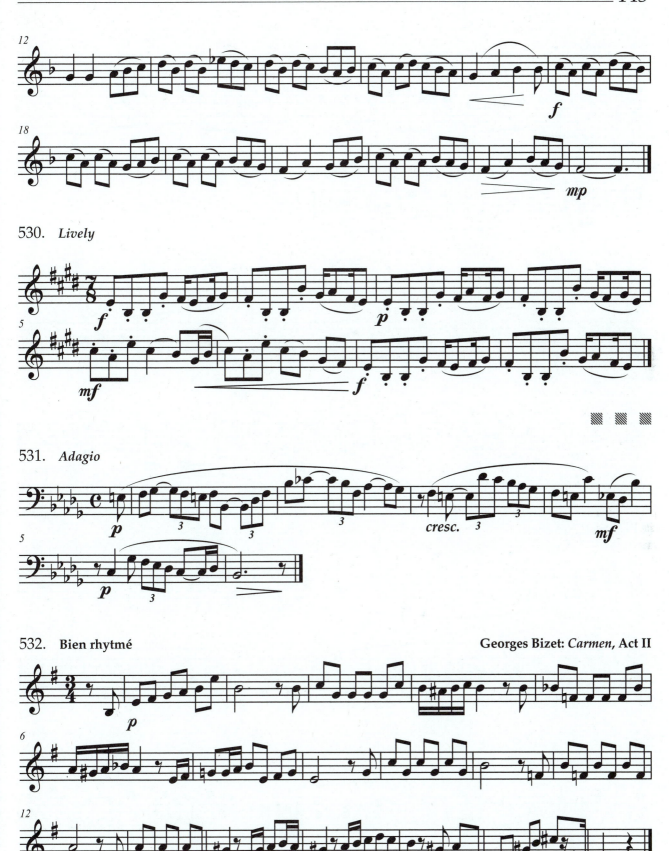

530. *Lively*

531. *Adagio*

532. **Bien rhytmé** **Georges Bizet:** *Carmen*, **Act II**

533. *Andante*

534. *Larghetto*

535. *Waltz* **(in one)**

536. *Andante con moto*

This example from Schubert's *Winterreise* includes a motion to III and VI.

537. **Mäßig**   **Schubert, "Gute Nacht" (harmony simplified)**

538. *Free and easy*

539. *Ländler*

540. *Valse brillante*

541. *Etwas gedehnt*

542. *Allegro*

543. *Andantino*

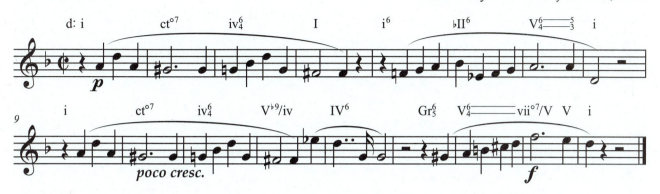

544. *Allegro deciso*

545. *Andantino*

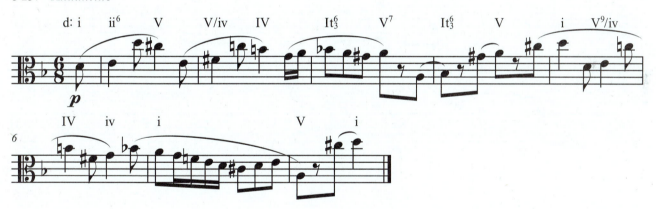

546. *Arietta—Andante*

(Continued)

546. *Arietta—Andante (Continued)*

547. *With movement*

548. *Grave*

549. *Lento ed espressivo*

550. *Allegro piacevole*

▨ ▨ ▨ The next three melodies include changing meters. See rhythm exercises 209–213 in Chapter Two for additional exercises featuring changing meters.

551. Lively

552. Misterioso

553. *Piacevole*

554. Moderato, Dance ♩ = 138

558. *Allegro moderato*

559. *Très vif et détaché*

560. *Andantino*

Rimsky-Korsakov: *Scheherazade*, II

561. *Allegro*

565. **Larghetto**

Beethoven: Violin Concerto, II

573. *Largo espressivo*

574. *Calore*

575. *Allegretto*

576. *Mazurka—Risoluto*

577. *Largo*

578. **Sehr mässig**   Hugo Wolf: "Nimmersatte Liebe" (*Möricke Lieder*, No. 9: adapted)

579. *Allegro*

580. *Tempo di marcia*

581. *Adagio*

582. Nicht zu geschwind

Schubert: *"Rückblick"* (harmony adapted)

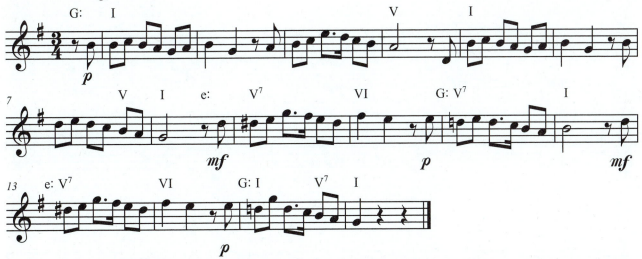

 The next four melodies pose new rhythmic challenges. For unusual subdivisions of the beat (for example, quintuplets), practice rhythm exercises beginning with exercise 219 in Chapter Two.

583. Lento

584. Dance!

585. *Espressif*

586. **Con moto**

The next three melodies begin and end in a different mode or key.

587. *Animato*

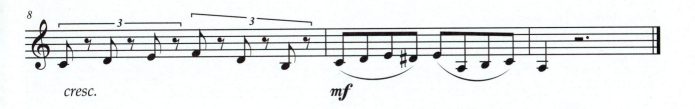

cresc.   *mf*

588. *Animé mais expressif*

589. *Gioviale*

590. *Andante ma con moto*

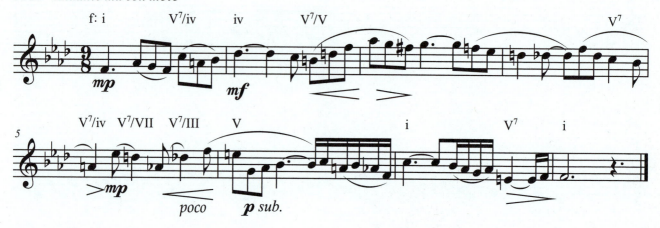

Major and minor modes are combined in the next eight melodies.

591. *Allegro con spirito*

592. *Allegretto*

593. **Gemütlich**

594. *Allegro*

595. *Allegro non tanto*

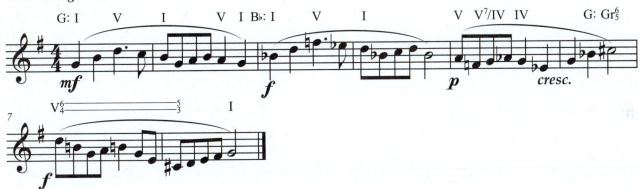

596. **Lebhaft**   **Brahms: "Frühlingslied" Sechs Lieder, Op. 85, No. 5 (adapted)**

597. **Langsam**

Brahms: "Sommerabend" Sechs Lieder, Op. 85, No. 1 (adapted)

598. *Tempo di minuetto*

599. *Expressively*

600. *Vif* (♪ = ♪)

601. *Andantino*

602. *Mässig und zart*

603. *Vivo*

604. *Con moto*

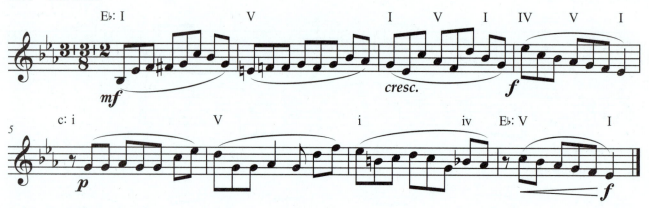

605. *With spirit*

606. *Lively*

607. *Spiritoso*

608. *Allegro gioviale*

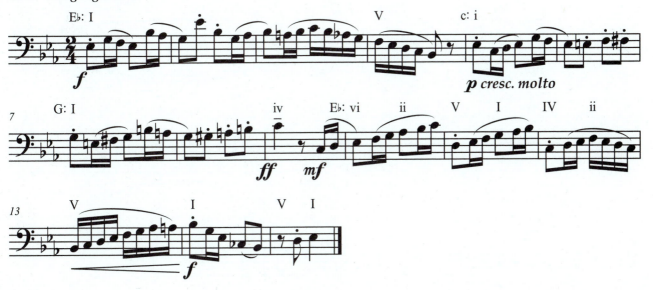

609. *Lebhaft und stark*

610. *Andante espressivo*

611. *Andantino*

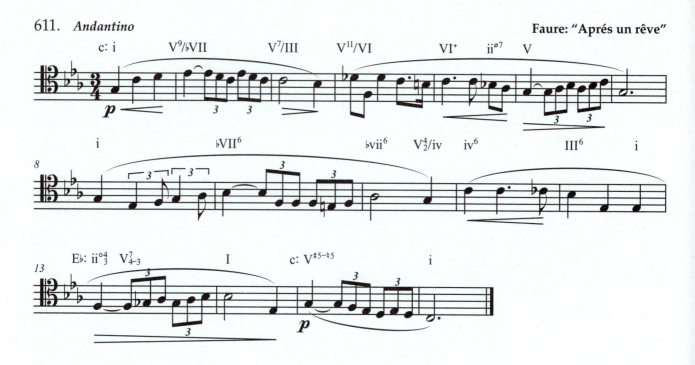

612. *Moderato*

613. *Allegro marcato*

619. *Allegretto*

620. *Vivo*

621. *Allegro con brio*

These last three melodies are from the twentieth century. They make a good transition to the melodies of Section V, in which tonal connections and patterns are no longer evident.

622. **Con moto**   **Béla Bartók,** *Mikrokosmos,* **No. 101, Vol. IV**

623. *Andante con moto* ♩ = **60**   **Stravinsky:** *The Rite of Spring,* **Part II**

624. *Lento* ♩ = **50**   **Stravinsky:** *The Rite of Spring,* **Part I**

MELODIES ▨ *SECTION V*

Post-Tonal Melodies

Singing post-tonal music is challenging, not only because our ears are less familiar with it than with tonal music (both classical and popular), which we hear ubiquitously, but also because intonation is weakened without the gravitational pull toward the central pitch (the tonic) so fundamental to the tonal scale or key. You will find that even singing half steps and whole steps in tune, generally so straightforward in the context of major and minor scales, is challenging without the anchoring influence of tonality. You should therefore work through each exercise slowly, concentrating on good pitch accuracy and intonation, building up speed with increased familiarity. The tempo or descriptive marking of each melody speaks to its character, and reflects an ideal tempo or "mood," although these descriptions are advisory. You should strive for accuracy, even if it means slowing down the tempo. All of the practice suggestions offered at the head of Chapter One, Section I can be heeded profitably here, with the exception of the maintenance of tonic in the singer's memory. As with the tonal melodies, you will advance more swiftly and surely by attempting to sound out the melodies with minimal aid of the piano or another instrument, checking pitch only on occasion. These exercises are written as melodies rather than as random successions of intervals, and, with practice, you will find these melodies memorable.

This section presents a variety of post-tonal styles, including music created from different methods of organization: free atonal, whole tone, octatonic, and serial methods. Although the music is not tonal, many of the exercises emphasize certain pitches—through repetition or through their structural placement—and a good pitch memory, and awareness of the organization within a melody, will help you hear and sing the examples. In addition, a sense of the larger line and an awareness of the connection between non-adjacent notes will be far more helpful than trying to sing each discrete interval.

The first several exercises introduce only minor and major seconds, while the next part adds perfect fourths. The section progresses in this way, adding one or two intervals at a time until every simple interval is introduced and practiced. (For convenience of reading, intervals are sometimes spelled enharmonically—for example, a major seventh as a diminished octave.) In this way, you will become familiar with the particular sound of each interval, and learn to reproduce it in any context, before moving on to the next.

Each part of Section V begins with a series of exercises that is designed so the student can rigorously practice the new interval or intervals. These should be sung at a slow, steady tempo. The exercises that follow integrate the new interval(s) into the fabric of the melodies. Each part concludes with melodies from the literature that contain both newly introduced intervals(s) and the previously studied intervals. These melodies come from composers whose styles vary widely, including twentieth-century works by composers such as Samuel Barber, Béla Bartók, Miriam Gideon, Hans Werner Henze, Henry Lazarof, Ruth Crawford Seeger, Claude Vivier and more recent music by composers writing today, including Martin Blessinger, David Froom, Piers Hellawell, among others. The variety of approaches to melody writing will prepare you to be able to sing at sight melodies from a broad variety of post-tonal works.

On occasion, an interval that has not yet been introduced may occur between two notes. In such cases, a dotted line is provided to connect the second note of one such interval with a previous note. Remembering the first note will help you sing the second note. In the example below, there is a diminished fifth between the B in the last note of measure three and the F beginning measure four. If you remember the G beginning in measure 2, you will be able to hear the M2 down to F at the beginning of measure 4. In most instances, the dotted line connects the same note or a note a m2 or M2 apart. On occasion, the dotted line connects two notes of a familiar interval.

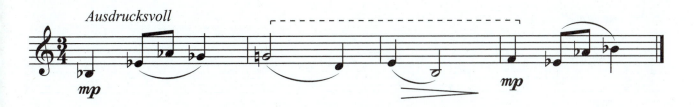

Part 1: Minor Seconds (m2) and Major Seconds (M2)

Only minor and major seconds are found in Part 1. Singing seconds in good intonation in tonal music, in the context of the gravitation toward tonic, is easier than singing them in a nontonal context. Sing the exercises slowly at first, playing the note you are singing on an instrument every so often to check intonation. As your skill increases, increase the tempo.

▨ ▨ ▨   The first two exercises consist of half steps only.

625.   *Slow and deliberate*

626.   *Slow and deliberate*

▨ ▨ ▨

▨ ▨ ▨   The next two exercises consist entirely of whole steps. Good sight singing requires quick recognition of intervals. Recognize that the last note of measure 4 and the first note of measure 5—G♯-B♭—spell a diminished third but sound like a whole step.

627.   *Andante*

628.   *Andante*

The remaining melodies in Part 1 contain minor and major seconds. The next three exercises are meant to be sung slowly, as a means to acquaint you with the process of determining the interval, hearing it, and then singing it. As your skill in determining/hearing/singing improves, so should your tempo increase. As new intervals are added in Section V, your skill in determining/hearing/singing motives will broaden and your skill increase. In Part 1, your challenge is to determine which intervals are minor and which are major seconds.

633. *Largo*

634. *Jaunty*

635. *Bewegt*

Octatonic scales have eight notes arranged in a pattern of alternating whole and half steps. The three octatonic scales:

 The next five exercises are created from octatonic scales.

636. *Moderato*

637. *Moderato*

638. *Flowing*

639. *Swaying*

*When adjacent notes create an interval that has not yet been covered, dotted lines connect a note with a prior note for reference. In this case, you are referred to the previous F as an aid to hearing the subsequent F. For more information, see the paragraph on dotted lines in the introduction to Section V on page 174.

640. *Andante con moto*

The following examples from the literature are comprised almost entirely of seconds. On the infrequent occasions where another interval appears, the dotted lines connect one of the notes to a previous note. In all cases here and in the subsequent parts, tempi are those indicated in the score. Some of these tempi will not be possible to sing. You are advised to work through the melodies slowly, and increase the tempo as much as possible to gain fluency. This will mean sometimes singing at a faster tempo than indicated, and sometimes at a slower tempo than indicated in the cases where the tempo is impossibly fast.

641.   **Claude Vivier:** *Lonely Child*

642.   **Harrison Birtwistle:** *9 Settings of Lorine Niedecker,* **IX**

643. *Pesante*   **Béla Bartók: Concerto for Orchestra, V**

*Original tempo; you will likely want to take it slower.

Part 2: Adding the Perfect Fourth (m2, M2, P4)

The first three exercises in this subsection are meant to be sung slowly. As your facility in recognizing, hearing, and then singing the interval increases, you will increase the tempo. Be on the lookout for opportunities to hear not just discrete intervals but connections between notes that are not adjacent and the contour of the melodic line.

644.

645.

646.

647. *Waltz*

648. *Deliberate*

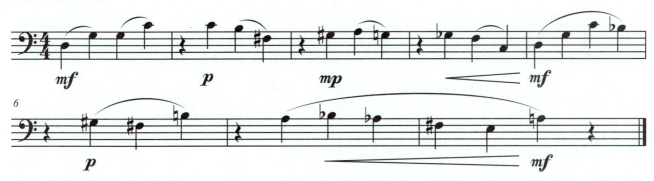

649. *Lilting*

650. *Allegretto*

651. *Dolente*

652. *Ausdrucksvoll*

653. *Animato*

654. *Adagio ed espressivo*

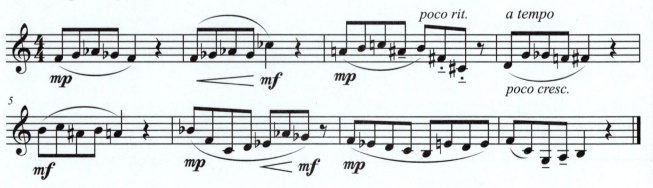

655. *Moderato*

656. *Moderately fast*

657. *Vif*

658. *Deciso*

659. *Lebhaft*

660.   **Hans Werner Henze:** *Versuch über Schweinen* **(adapted)**

661. *Tranquillo*   **Ruth Crawford Seeger: Five Songs, II**

662.   **Béla Bartók: Concerto for Orchestra, I (adapted)**

663.

Béla Bartók: Concerto for Orchestra, I

Part 3: Adding the Perfect Fifth (m2, M2, P4, P5)

Students often have difficulty distinguishing between perfect fourths and perfect fifths, especially when these intervals are descending. The following melodies offer ample descending perfect fourths and fifths (ascending as well) so that students can practice hearing the difference and singing them accurately. In addition, a good warm-up exercise is picking a note and singing two or three perfect fourths ascending, following by picking another note and singing two or three perfect fourths descending. Do this several times, choosing different notes. Do the same with perfect fifths. The ability to hear and sing ascending and descending perfect fourths and perfect fifths reliably starting on any note will assist in singing the following melodies.

 The first three exercises in this subsection are to be sung slowly. As your comfort identifying/ hearing/singing perfect fifths increases, your tempo may also increase. See if you can scan the line, noting what you just sang and what you are about to sing. Such awareness will assist you in making connections between nonadjacent notes.

664.

665.

666. *Getragen*

667. *Grazioso*

668. *Ruhig*

669. *Eroica*

670. *Sprightly*

671. *Tempo di valse*

672. *Moderately fast but with expression*

673. *Spiritoso*

674. *Vif*

675. *Playful*

676. *Lugubre*

677. *Barcarole*

678. *Andante espressivo*

679. *Risoluto e pesante*   Béla Bartók: *Mikrokosmos*, 83

680.   Béla Bartók: Concerto for Orchestra, I

681.   Béla Bartók: Concerto for Orchestra, IV

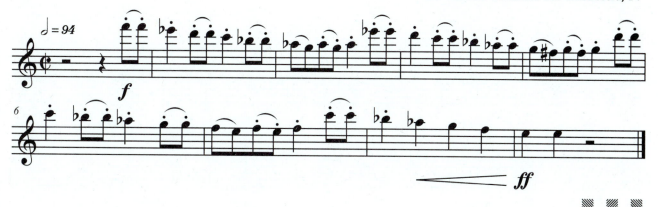

Part 4: Adding Minor Third and Major Third (m2, M2, m3, M3, P4, P5)

Sing the first three exercises in this sub-section slowly. Be especially aware of the difference between minor 3rds and major 3rds as you identify/"hear"/and sing each interval.

682.

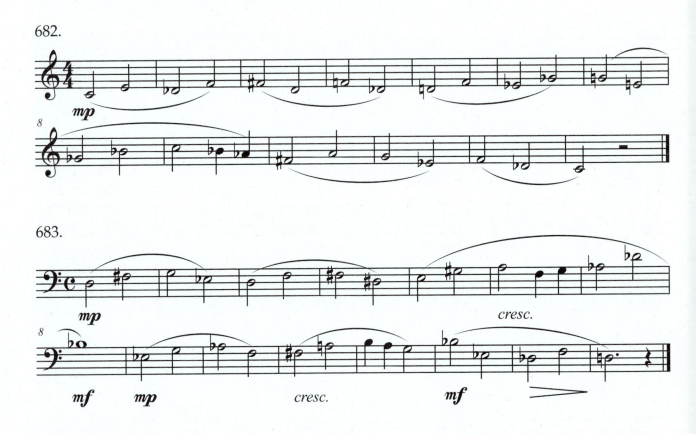

When sight singing, it is always helpful to look at the harmonic context rather than thinking in single discrete intervals. In many of the melodies that follow, successions of thirds create major, minor, diminished, and augmented triads. While reading successive thirds, if you discern the quality of the triad (major, minor, diminished, or augmented), you will have a sonority in mind as you sing the pitches.

684.

685. *Moderato*

686. *Deciso*

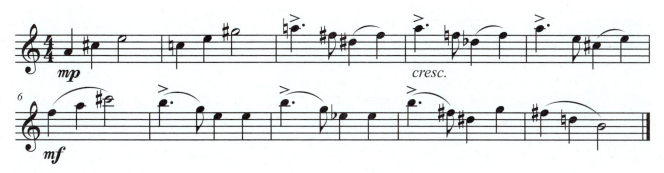

687. *Langsam und zart*

688. *Lebhaft*

689. *Andante*

690. *Con moto*

691. *Jaunty*

692. *Swaying*

693. Tranquillo

694. Affretando

695. Moderato

696. Allegro commodo

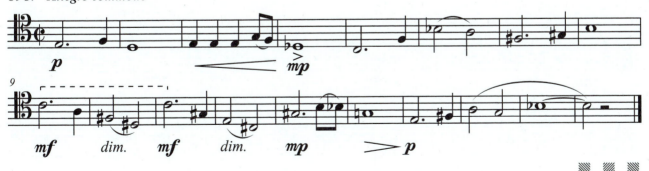

697. *Molto adagio*   **Samuel Barber:** *Hermit Songs,* "Church Bell at Night"

698. *Allegro*   **Edward Smaldone:** "June 2011"

699. *Andante tranquillo*   **Béla Bartók:** *Music for Strings, Percussion, and Celesta,* I

700.   **David Froom: "Flamboyan," from** *Three Love Songs on Poetry of Sue Standing* **(adapted)**

701. *Slow, Legato*   **Martin Blessinger: "Escapes," from** *Diversions and Escapes* **(adapted)**

Part 5: Adding Tritones—Augmented Fourths and Diminished Fifths (m2, M2, m3, M3, P4, TT, P5)

To sight sing proficiently, it is essential that you correctly identify every interval. Doing so will increase the accuracy with which you sing. Additionally, "keeping track" of important or memorable pitches will aid you in hearing later ones. For example, if you remember the starting pitch, "C," in the first exercise, hearing "D" in m. 4 will be easier. Hearing the "D" in relationship to the "C" may help you hear the "E♭" in m. 2. Sing the first three exercises slowly, increasing the tempo as you become more comfortable with the tritones.

702.

703.

704.

705. *Largo*

706. *Largo*

707. *Marziale*

708. *Comodo*

709. *Valse*

710. *Valse macabre*

711. *Drammatico*

712. *Deliberate*

713. *Giocoso*

714. *Gustoso*

715. *Flowing*

716. *Allegretto gioviale*

 The next two melodies are composed using twelve-tone rows.

717. *Teneramente*

718. *Deliberate*

With the addition of the tritone, we now have seven of the twelve possible simple intervals (intervals of an octave or less) in our vocabulary. It is a good time to reiterate that successful sight singing depends upon the quick calculation of the interval while also understanding the context. Continue practicing looking backward (and forward) as you read, taking advantage of memorable repeated pitches, pitches at the beginnings of phrases, low and high pitch points, etc. In the next example, by Hans Werner Henze, when you come to measure 3, it is much easier to remember the E♭ as the first note you sang rather than calculating and "hearing" the diminished fourth between the previous B in measure 2 and the E♭ that begins m. 3. Similarly, in the following melody, by Béla Bartók, it is far easier in measure 2 to hear the E as the first note you sang than to hear the E as a descending tritone from A♯. Practice hearing and remembering notes, and developing strategies as you sing so that you do not approach the music as a string of discrete intervals with no connection to their surrounding context.

719.   **Hans Werner Henze:** *Being Beauteous*

720. *Allegretto*   **Béla Bartòk: Concerto for Orchestra, IV**

721. *Quasi Parlando*   **Piers Hellawell: "Memorandum II" from *Isabella's Banquet***

Part 6: Adding Minor Sixth and Major Sixth (m2, M2, m3, M3, P4, TT, P5, m6, M6)

The first three exercises are to be sung slowly. Increase the tempo as you get the sound of the minor and major sixths in your ears. As always, retain pitches at important structural points in the middle (such as the beginnings and ends of phrases) as well as high and low pitches, which tend to be memorable with concentration. For example, in the next exercise, retain the begining "A" in m. 1 to assist you in singing the "A" in m. 2.

722.

723.

724. *Allegro commodo*

725. *Langsam*

726. *Gemütlich*

727. *Affettuoso*

728. *Flowing*

729. *Melancholy*

730. *Lusingando*

731. **Cheerful and with movement**

732. **Plaintive**

733. **Piacevole**

734. *Langsam*

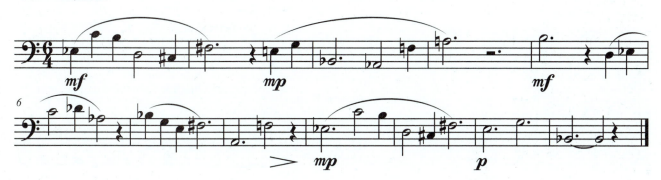

The next two melodies are composed using twelve-tone rows.

735. *Moderato*

736. *Marziale*

737. *Lento*   **Hans Werner Henze:** *Kammermusik 1958*

738.

Henri Lazarof: *"Encounters" with Dylan Thomas,* **III**

739.

Miriam Gideon: *Spirit above the Dust,* **VI**

Part 7: Adding the Minor Seventh and Major Seventh (m2, M2, m3, M3, P4, TT, P5, m6, M6, m7, M7)

With the addition of the minor and major seventh, we come to the largest intervals we have encountered so far and complete the entire collection of "simple" intervals. To get the sevenths into your ear, sing the preparatory exercises below. With practice, you will internalize the transfer of register and hear and sing the seventh with confidence.

Try these exercises on different pitches besides the ones given below. Try both approaches to see which one works best for you while you are learning how to sing the sevenths more immediately and automatically.

PREPARATORY EXERCISES:
To sing each seventh, imagine the succession of notes that includes the grace note.

When you can internalize the sound of the grace note, you can sing the seventh without it.

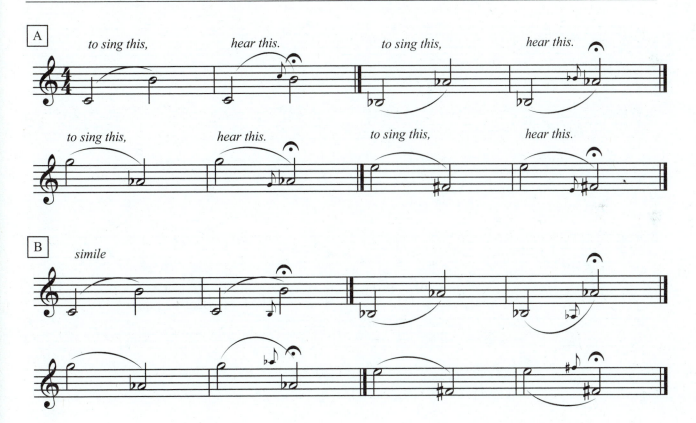

Sing the next three exercises slowly and deliberately to practice hearing and singing the sevenths. Increase the tempo as you get the sound of the sevenths in your ears.

740.

741.

742.

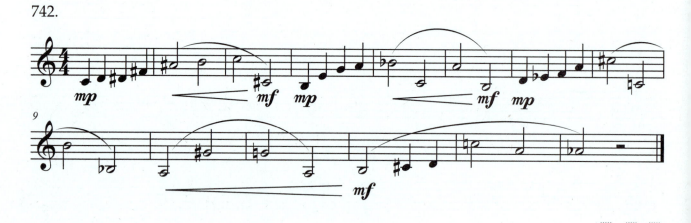

743. **Zart**

744. *Vivo*

745. *Playful*

746. *Playful but not too fast*

747. *Steady and with movement*

748. *Andante*

749. *Deliberately and emphatically*

750. *Brisk*

751. *Rocking*

752. *Deliberatamente*

The next two melodies are composed using twelve-tone rows.

753. *Doloroso*

754. *Adagio*

755. *Allegro con brio*   **Ruth Crawford Seeger: Five Songs, V**

[cresc. poco a poco]

756. **With edgy energy throughout**   Perry Goldstein: *Late Night Thoughts from the V.A.*, **III (adapted)**

757.   **Hans Werner Henze:** *Being Beauteous*

CHAPTER TWO

Rhythm

A solid rhythmic sense is a crucial feature of good musicianship, and conducting exercises as you sing them will help you hone your sense of rhythm. The conducting pattern (see p. 2) identifies the beat, and places the beat within the meter. This will help you interpret the relationship between the written notation and its realization in sound. When singing melodies and duets, or singing and playing the piano, you must coordinate all aspects of musical performance: pitch, rhythm, phrasing, intonation, dynamics, articulation, etc. The exercises in this chapter isolate and drill specific rhythmic and metric patterns and concepts to increase your rhythmic facility and improve your musical performance and reading skills.

Isolated practice in rhythm is not an end in itself. For that reason (and to increase the usefulness of the exercises), the rhythmic exercises are notated without tempo indications, dynamics, etc. You should vary tempos, performing the same exercise at a variety of tempi. Many melodies in Chapter One direct you to specific rhythm exercises for related practice, and all of the melody and duet materials can be vocalized or tapped as rhythm exercises. Confident rhythmic articulation and a good sense of time provide the foundation for artful and musical phrasing. The goal of musicianship training is to perform the music of the printed page with the appropriate balance of grounded rhythm and flexible phrasing. These are the hallmarks of good musical performance.

RHYTHM ▨ *SECTION I*

To be used with Section I of all other chapters

The essential elements in the study of rhythm are the development of the concept of the beat, how that beat is notated in a particular meter, and how the surface rhythms relate to that beat. The first exercises in this section are confined to three basic rhythms: the quarter note, two eighths, and the quarter rest. The beat is represented by the shaded area. Conduct each exercise. As an introduction to conducting, you can tap the desk or table with your right hand. Each tap should represent one beat, or one shaded box. Conducting with a pattern of 2, 3, or 4 is simply a matter of applying the appropriate direction to the "tap." For conducting diagrams, see page 2.

6.

7.

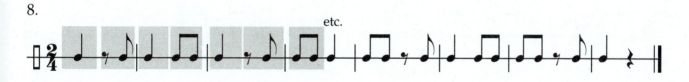
The next group of exercises adds the eighth rest and eighth note to the existing patterns. Feel free to add boxes to the notation to help coordinate conducting and singing.

8.

etc.

This rhythm repeats the previous one, but the notation makes it harder to see the relationship between the beats and rhythms. If you box the beats, do so carefully to show how the flagged eighth notes occupy the second half of the boxes, and the second half of the beat.

9.

etc.

10.

11.

12.

The next exercise repeats the attack points of the previous one, with some of the rhythms notated differently.

13.

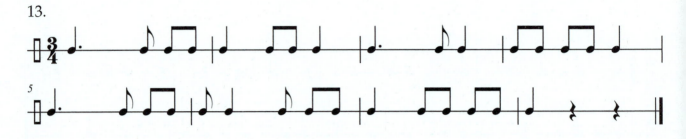

14.

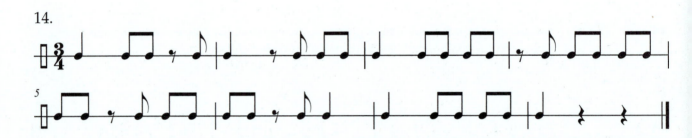

If you are having trouble with the conducting pattern, try tapping the same spot on your desk as you "sing" the rhythms. When you are comfortable with this, try moving your hand in the appropriate direction as you tap, then switch to the conducting pattern without tapping. See page 2 for conducting diagrams.

The next exercise can be performed as a four-part round. (Each voice enters at four-measure intervals.)

15.

16.

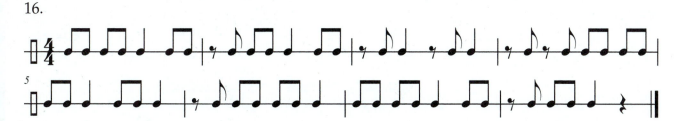

17.

▨ ▨ ▨ The next exercises introduce new subdivisions of the quarter note. For now, these will consist of four sixteenths, an eighth and two sixteenths, or a dotted eighth and sixteenth in simple time. Make sure you connect the rhythms with the shaded beats in your imagination.

18.

▨ ▨ ▨ Here we encounter a half note, which gets two beats in this time signature. Notice how this changes later when we encounter the half note in cut time.

19.

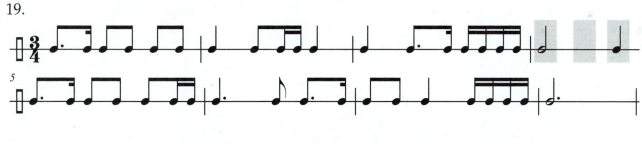

20.

21.

22.

23.

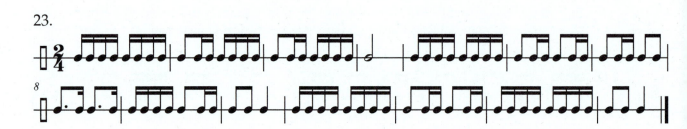

▧ ▨ ▩ All of the exercises to this point have been based on meters in which the quarter note gets the beat. The eighth note gets the beat in the next seven examples. Notice how the beat and the shaded box are transferred to a different rhythmic value, but function the same way.

24.

25.

26.

▨ ▨ ▨ Make sure you conduct the next two exercises in three. Notice how the sixteenth rest has the same relationship to the beat as the eighth rest did in meters where the quarter note gets the beat. Compare exercise 28 with exercise 12.

27.

28.

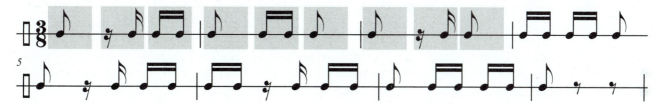

29. *Conduct in four.*

30.

▨ ▨ ▨ Conduct the next exercise in two. Notice how you have to shift your focus to make the quarter note the beat. The single beat pattern now includes division into four, in this case four sixteenths. What is the comparable rhythmic value in $\frac{2}{8}$? Compare exercises 31 and 32.

31.

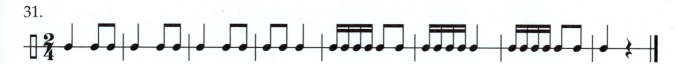

32.

Cut time should be conducted in two with the beat as the half note; compare the sound and the notation of this exercise with the previous two exercises. As an exercise, three students can simultaneously perform examples 31, 32, and 33.

33.

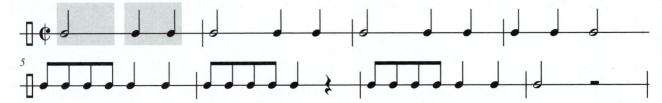

Notice how the quarter rest and quarter note divide the beat in measure 2 and elsewhere. Compare how this relationship between the rhythm and the beat is notated in exercises 8 and 28. Conduct this in two.

34.

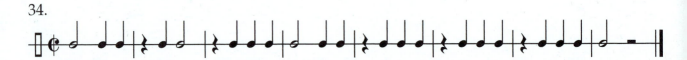

35.

Notice how the dotted quarter and eighth fit into a single beat in cut time. The next three exercises include all of the beat divisions studied so far.

36.

37.

38.

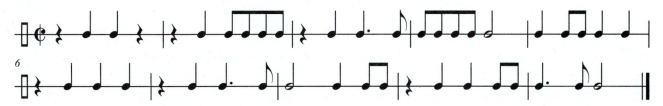

▨ ▨ ▨ $\frac{6}{8}$ is a compound meter, which means that the beat divides into three equal parts. In $\frac{6}{8}$ time, the dotted quarter note gets the beat, which is subdivided into three eighth notes.

39.

▨ ▨ ▨ Box each beat to help focus your eye on the relationship of the notation to the sound of the rhythm. Do this whenever you need to.

40.

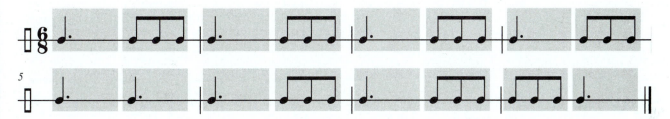

▨ ▨ ▨ The dotted quarter note beat can also be divided into a quarter note and an eighth note, creating a long-short division of the beat.

41.

42.

▨ ▨ ▨ This exercise can be combined with exercise 41 or 42 to create a duet.

43.

 This exercise incorporates the eighth rest.

44.

This exercise combines the previously studied rhythms and includes the eighth rest in a new context.

45.

Now the eighth rest is found on any one of the three subdivisions of the dotted eighth.

46.

Make sure you can see the dotted quarter beat in relation to the various patterns that include rests.

47.

5

48.

 In the next example, notice how the tie "substitutes" for the rest.

49.

▨ ▨ ▨ In the next example, isolate and drill the new dotted rhythm in measure 1, and the new sixteenth note rhythm in measure 5. Sing each of these measures repeatedly until you are comfortable, then sing the entire exercise. Note how the sixteenths divide the eighths within the larger beat. Conduct the dotted quarter note.

50.

51.

52.

▨ ▨ ▨ The next exercises introduce the pick-up. Make sure your conducting pattern coincides with the pick-up.

53.

54.

▨ ▨ ▨ In the next two exercises, the pick-up is less than a full beat in length.

55.

56.

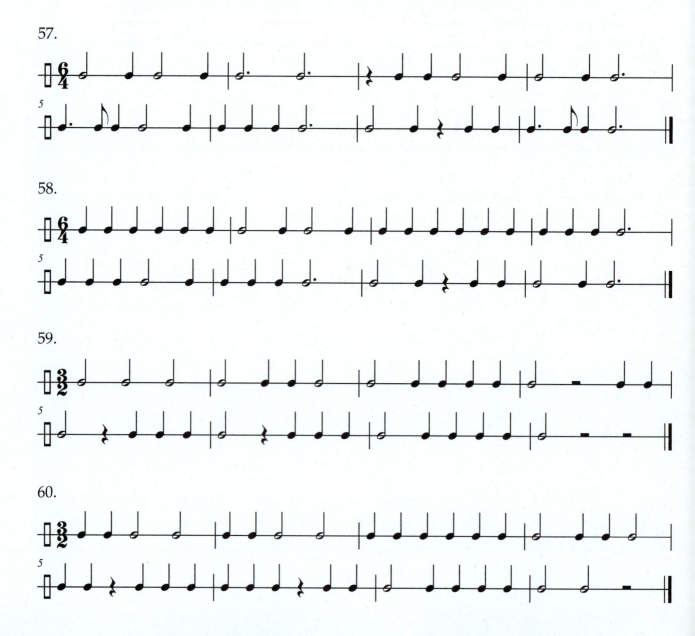

The next six examples introduce the time signatures of $^6_4$, $^3_2$, and $^4_2$. The normal conducting pattern for $^6_4$ is "in two," where the dotted half-note gets one beat. Without beams, it can be challenging to "see" how the rhythms coordinate with the beat. Take a pencil and mark the beginning of each large beat if needed. Notice that the sound of the rhythms, and the relation of those rhythms to the overall beat, is similar to $^6_8$. For the time signatures of $^3_2$ and $^4_2$, the beat is the half-note, which is the same as cut-time. These exercises should be performed at a variety of tempi.

57.

58.

59.

60.

61.

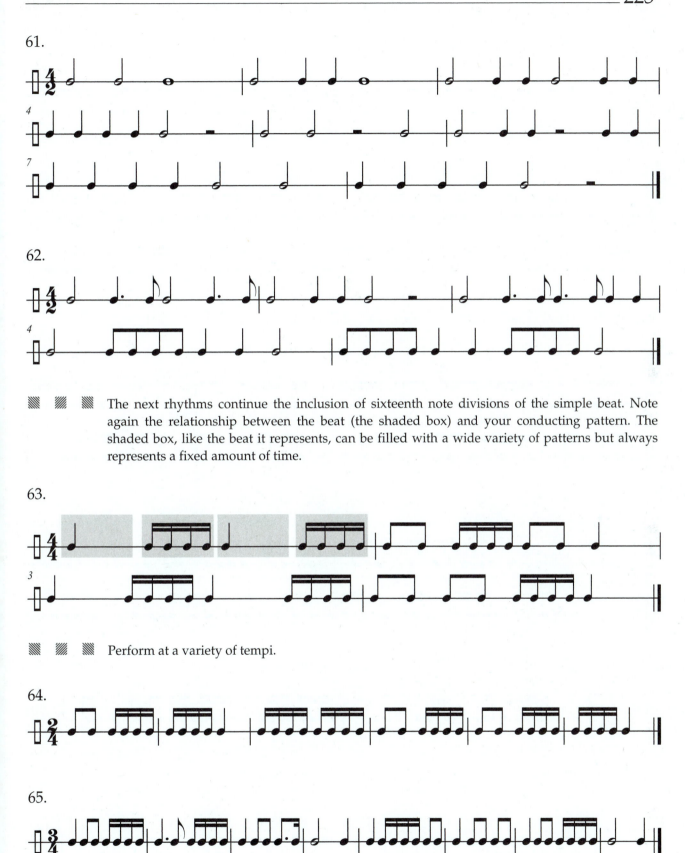

62.

The next rhythms continue the inclusion of sixteenth note divisions of the simple beat. Note again the relationship between the beat (the shaded box) and your conducting pattern. The shaded box, like the beat it represents, can be filled with a wide variety of patterns but always represents a fixed amount of time.

63.

Perform at a variety of tempi.

64.

65.

 Now we add the pattern of an eighth and two sixteenths to previous patterns.

66.

67.

68. The next three exercises incorporate eighth and quarter rests.

69.

70.

The next three exercises incorporate the dotted quarter and the dotted eighth.

71.

72.

73.

The next exercises apply similar beat divisions to cut time. Always conduct cut time in two! Apply the concepts learned in these rhythm exercises to melodic examples with similar rhythms. Any of the melodies in the book can thus serve as an additional rhythm exercise.

74.

75.

76.

▨ ▨ ▨ Notice the difference between the eighth rest and the quarter rest in the next exercise.

77.

▨ ▨ ▨ The next seven exercises summarize all of the rhythmic topics of this section. In addition to being a summary of Section 1, these exercises can serve as a "warm-up" before embarking on the new topics of the next section. This is a good opportunity to make sure that your conducting pattern is carefully coordinated with your performance.

78.

79.

80.

81.

82.

83.

84.

To be used with Section II of all other chapters

The time signatures $\frac{9}{8}$ and $\frac{12}{8}$ follow the same principles of beat and beat divisions as $\frac{6}{8}$: typically, the dotted quarter gets the beat. $\frac{9}{8}$ is typically three beats of a dotted quarter, and $\frac{12}{8}$ is four such beats. Add boxes to orient yourself while studying these examples.

85.

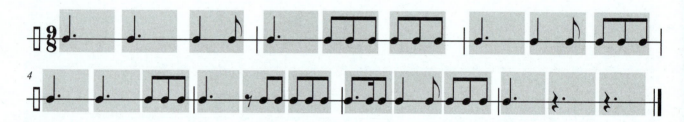

▨ ▨ ▨ In a meter like $\frac{9}{8}$ (or $\frac{12}{8}$), you may encounter a dotted half note, which gets two beats, and will therefore be two shaded boxes in length.

86.

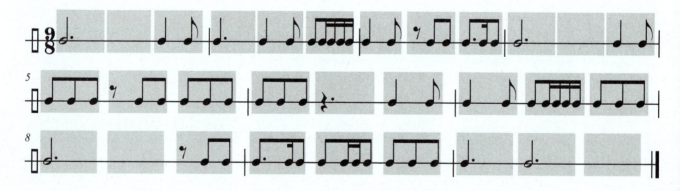

▨ ▨ ▨   Conduct ¹²⁄₈ just like ⁴⁄₄. Add boxes if you are having trouble visualizing how the meter is organized into beats. Notice that this rhythm starts with an upbeat.

87.

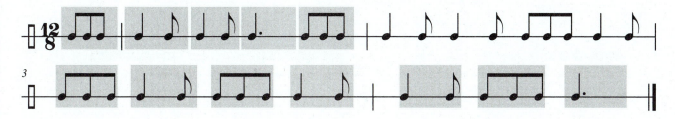

▨ ▨ ▨   Like example 87, the next exercise starts with an incomplete measure. On which beat does it begin? The next several exercises include eighth rests within the compound beat and the dotted quarter rest. Try to see where the boxes would be without adding them.

88.

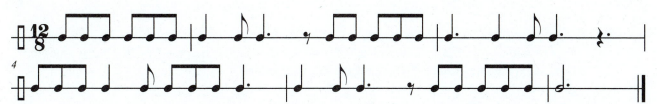

▨ ▨ ▨   As an alternative to boxes, draw a short line to focus your attention on the beginning of each beat.

89.

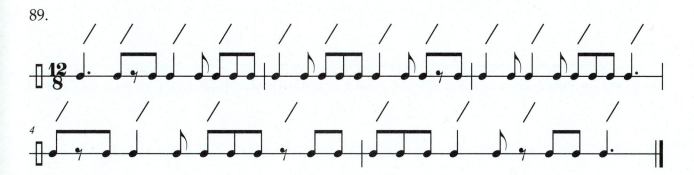

▨ ▨ ▨   Where would you draw the lines on the next exercise?

90.

▨ ▨ ▨ The next compound meter exercises explore a wider variety of the sixteenth note divisions. Note how the rhythms correspond to the conducting pattern, and make sure you see the relationship between the beat length and the rhythm. Here, we add six sixteenths, filling the compound beat.

91.

▨ ▨ ▨ Using different syllables for sixteenth notes makes them much easier to articulate, especially at faster tempi. Groups of four can be voiced with *ta-ka-ta-ka*.

92.

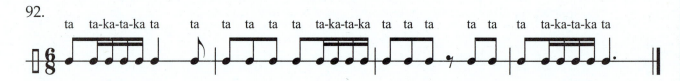

▨ ▨ ▨ Pairs of sixteenths divide the eighth note. Sing *ta-ka* for these pairs. When you alternate *ta* and *ka*, *ta* should always fall on a downbeat. These exercises should be practiced at a variety of tempi. Clean articulation can be challenging at very fast tempi.

93.

▨ ▨ ▨ The next exercise combines the subdivisions of the last three exercises with the eighth rest.

94.

▨ ▨ ▨ The same beat patterns can be applied to the compound beat of ⁹⁄₈. Conduct in three.

95.

Here we practice the dotted eighth-sixteenth pattern. Notice how the second eighth note of the compound beat is divided.

96.

Now try singing the previous rhythm using the syllables *ta-ka-ta* for the dotted eighth-sixteenth-eighth pattern. Using different syllables on sixteenths allows for easier articulation, especially in faster tempi. How would you apply the the syllables *ta* and *ka* to the next rhythm?

97.

The same concepts are here applied to $\frac{12}{8}$.

98.

Next, we combine the dotted eighth with additional sixteenth note patterns. The three sixteenths in measure 3 (and similar patterns) should be voiced with *ka-ta-ka*, which allows the syllable *ta* to land on the downbeat.

99.

100.

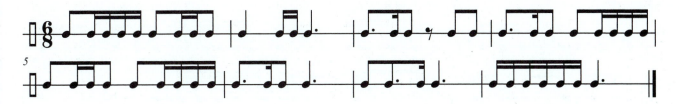

101.

In compound time signatures such as $\frac{6}{16}$ or $\frac{9}{16}$ the dotted eighth note gets the beat. Notice the relationship between the beat and its subdivisions.

102.

103.

104.

Which conducting pattern would you expect to use for $\frac{9}{16}$?

105.

106.

107.

▨ ▨ ▨   The next exercises introduce the eighth-note triplet in simple meters. The triplet divides into three a beat that normally divides into two. Hear the different ways the beat can be divided.

108.

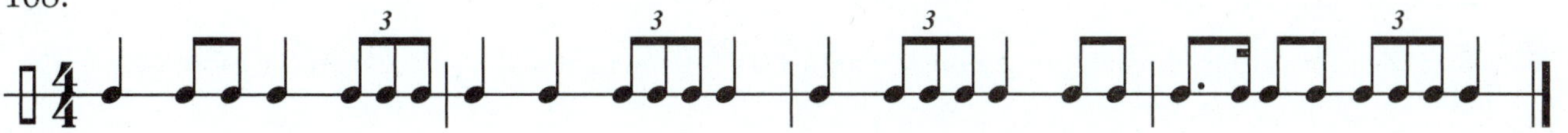

109.

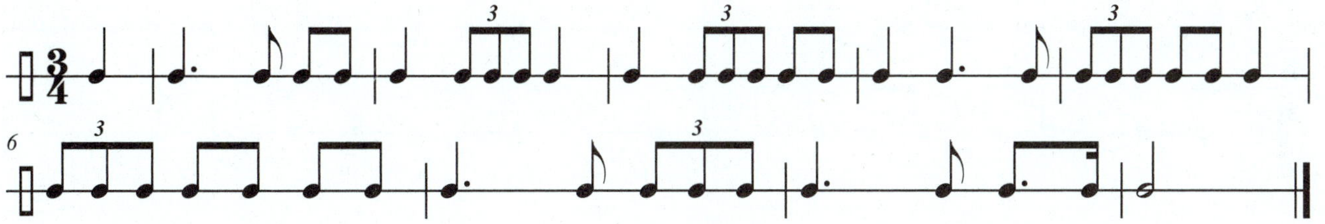

110.

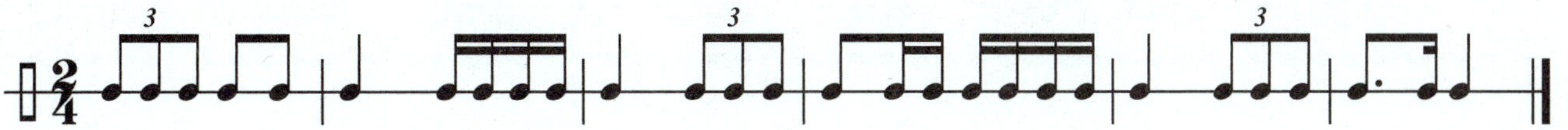

111.

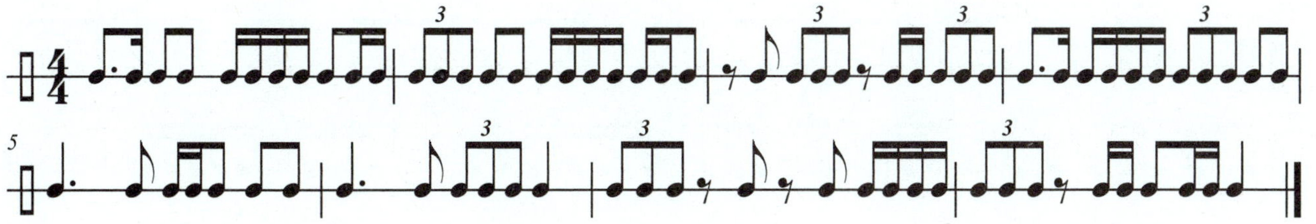

▨ ▨ ▨   Whereas the previous example requires the performer to switch between dividing the beat into two and three, the next exercise requires doing both simultaneously. Try tapping the next two exercises in a variety of manners: tap with both hands; sing one part and tap the other; tap one part while a partner taps the other. Coordinating two against three creates a recognizable composite rhythm. No matter how you perform two against three, the composite rhythm you should hear is the ostinato rhythm of the Christmas tune "Carol of the Bells."

112.

113.

▨ ▨ ▨   The next three exercises continue exploring the tie, which will now be included more frequently.

114.

115.

116.

▨ ▨ ▨ Notice how the different upbeats relate to the conducting patterns of the next five exercises.

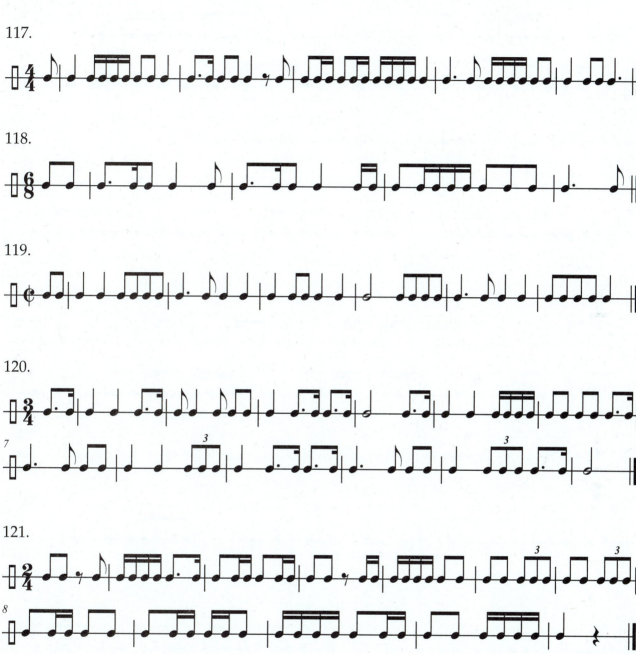

The next exercises introduce syncopation. Syncopation occurs when a typically unstressed beat or division of a beat receives a rhythmic stress. First, we notate a common syncopation using an eighth-quarter-eighth pattern in $\frac{2}{4}$. Notice how the syncopation relates to your conducting pattern.

123.

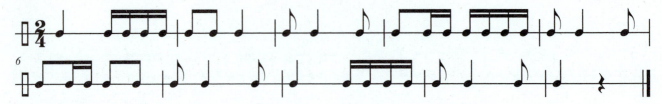

 The next exercises apply this syncopation to a variety of meters.

124.

125.

 Notice how the syncopation is notated in cut time. Conduct half notes.

126.

127.

128.

Notice how syncopations are created with ties.

129.

130.

131.

132.

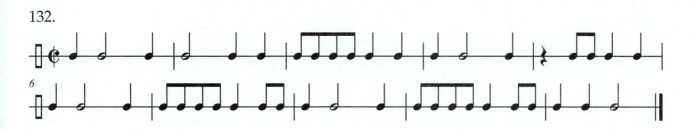

The next two examples include a syncopation contained within a single beat.

133.

134.

▧ ▨ ▧ Now these syncopated patterns are included in a variety of meters.

135.

136.

137.

138.

139.

▧ ▨ ▧ Notice how the two different syncopations are notated in cut time and $\frac{3}{2}$.

140.

▧ ▨ ▧   Notice how the half-note beat in the next example relates to the half-note beat of cut time.

141.

▧ ▨ ▧   Try this exercise at both fast and slow tempi. How would you distribute the syllables *ta* and *ka* to facilitate articulation in a fast tempo?

142.

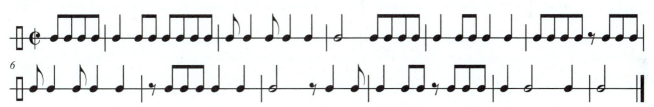

▧ ▨ ▧   The next exercises add ties to previously studied patterns. Note how maintaining your conducting pattern and visualizing the beat aids in the accurate performance of these ties.

143.

144.

If necessary, practice an example like the next one first without performing the ties, then with the ties included.

145.

146.

147.

148.

Conduct this in a fast tempo, one beat per measure. How fast can you perform this exercise?

149.

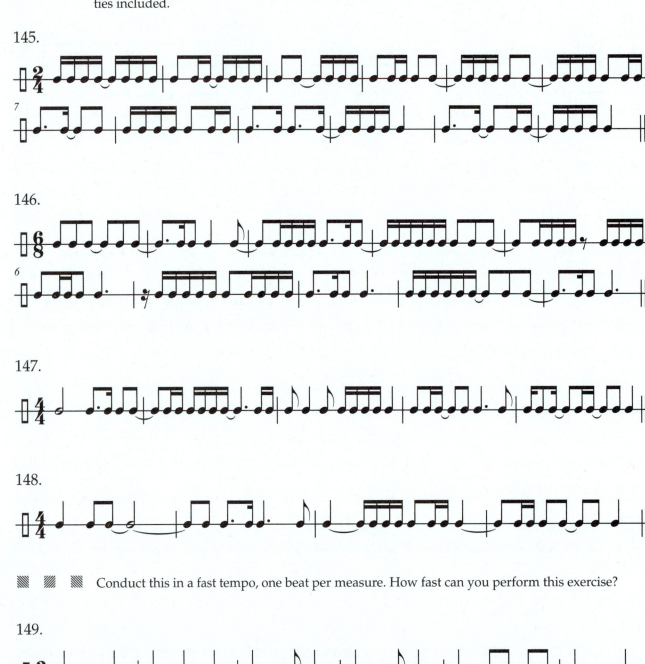

The presence of sixteenth note values implies a slower half note beat, but you should still conduct this in two.

150.

The next three exercises are the same, except for the placement of ties.

151.

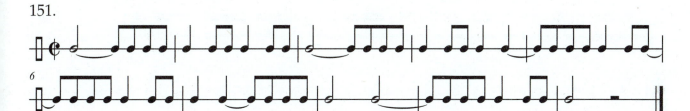

152.

153.

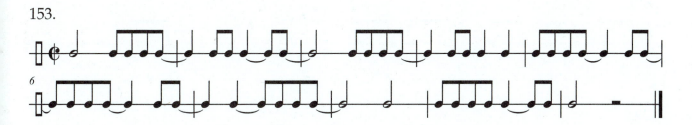

Experiment by adding some additional ties to this rhythm.

154.

155.

156.

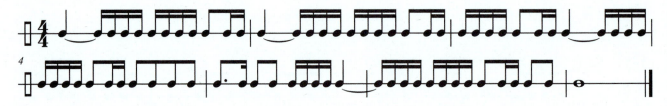

▨ ▨ ▨   Make sure the pick-up corresponds to the correct part of the conducting beat pattern.

157.

158.

159.

▨ ▨ ▨ Notice the eight-quarter combination in the next example. Make sure you see the beat correctly. Adding boxes might help.

160.

161.

162.

▨ ▨ ▨ Practice this exercise at a slow tempo to better recognize the distinctions between the beat divided into four sixteenths and into three triplets.

163.

164.

165.

166.

RHYTHM ▧ *SECTION III*

To be used with Section III of all other chapters

▧ ▨ ▧ The next exercise introduces the quarter note triplet in cut time. Notice how this rhythm corresponds to the half note beat.

167.

168.

▧ ▨ ▧ This is the same as the previous rhythm, but with some added ties.

169.

▧ ▨ ▧ Now the quarter note triplet is heard against two beats.

170.

171.

Here the quarter note triplet appears in an alternate notation, which clarifies the relationship of each quarter note triplet to the quarter note beat.

172.

Now ties are added.

173.

The next two exercises can be performed together as a duet.

174.

175.

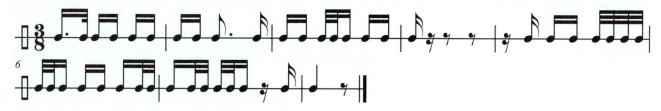

Pay close attention to the new value of the beat.

176.

177.

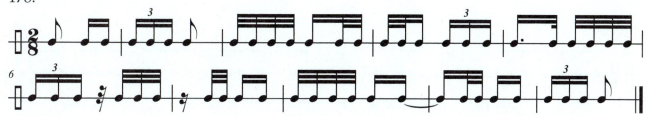

178.

179.

Here the dotted rhythm adds a new subdivision. Eighth-note and quarter-note triplets are included.

180.

181.

☒ ▨ ☒ Careful placement of *ta* and *ka* syllables will help on the next two exercises. Use *ka* on the second sixteenth of any divided eighth note.

182.

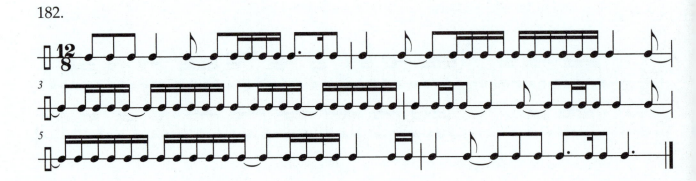

183.

☒ ▨ ☒ You can still use the concept of the shaded box to show the relationship between the beat and the rhythm that divides it. Make sure you conduct the quarter note in these exercises.

184.

185.

Conduct in two.

186.

187.

Conduct $\frac{3}{2}$ in three.

188.

189.

▨ ▨ ▨ $\frac{6}{4}$ is normally conducted in two. Which note value gets the beat? How would you add boxes on this and the previous exercise to show how the beats are organized?

190.

191.

▨ ▨ ▨ The following rhythms include some new divisions and syncopations in compound meters. Try to look ahead so that you can hear the rhythm before you articulate it.

192.

193.

▨ ▨ ▨ $\frac{5}{8}$, $\frac{7}{8}$, and other irregular meters typically combine simple and compound beats. $\frac{6}{8}$ and $\frac{9}{8}$ can be conducted using standard patterns for 2 and 3. For $\frac{5}{8}$, start by practicing the conducting pattern with one long and one short beat (either long+short or short+long). This can be counted 1-2 1-2-3, 1-2 1-2-3 or 1-2-3 1-2, 1-2-3 1-2, depending on the particular grouping of notes in the music you are performing. Compare the beat lengths of the next two exercises.

194.

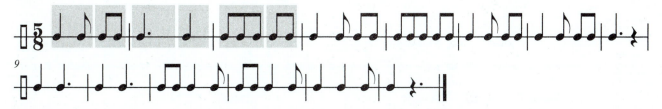

※ ※ ※ Now these beats (of either two or three eighths) are divided into familiar patterns.

195.

196.

※ ※ ※ Conduct $\frac{7}{8}$ in three, with one long and two short beats.

197.

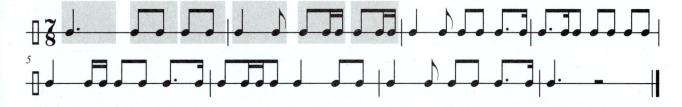

198.

Notice how the long beat is not always the first beat.

199.

200.

$\frac{5}{4}$ can also be conducted in two, if one beat is a dotted half note and the other is a half note. However, it is more difficult to see where the beat divisions are. $\frac{5}{4}$ can also be conducted by beating each of the five beats of the measure. This is usually done with a pattern that is like a $\frac{4}{4}$ pattern, with two "second beats." Try conducting each of these $\frac{5}{4}$ examples using a five-beat pattern, and also using a two-beat pattern.

201.

202.

203.

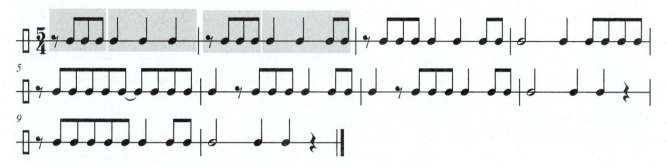

The many possible subdivisions in the next examples can be a challenge to the eye and to the ear. Keep your focus on the beat and how it fits into the meter. In this way, all of the subdivisions have a clear context for their performance. Often, a meter such as $\frac{4}{8}$ is used for a very slow tempo with elaborate subdivisions.

204.

205.

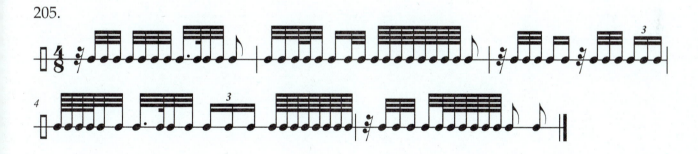

206.

▧ ▧ ▧   Conduct in two.

207.

208.

RHYTHM ▨ SECTION IV

To be used with Section IV of all other chapters

The rhythmic exercises in this section explore a number of advanced skills. However, the best way to develop advanced rhythmic skills is to incorporate those skills into an advanced musical performance, and therefore these exercises are not exhaustive. The challenging rhythms of the melodies, sing-and-play exercises, and duets in Section IV are therefore recommended to develop strong rhythmic skills.

▨ ▨ ▨ The following five exercises combine compound, simple, and irregular meters. Notice how each beat is notated to show the implied pattern of long and short beats. Typically, in music of changing meters like this, one rhythmic value remains constant. In the case of the next five exercises, the eighth note remains constant. Always conduct!

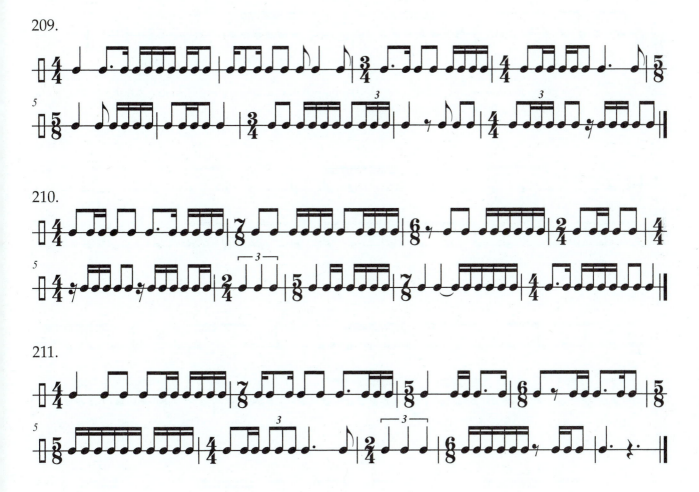

212.

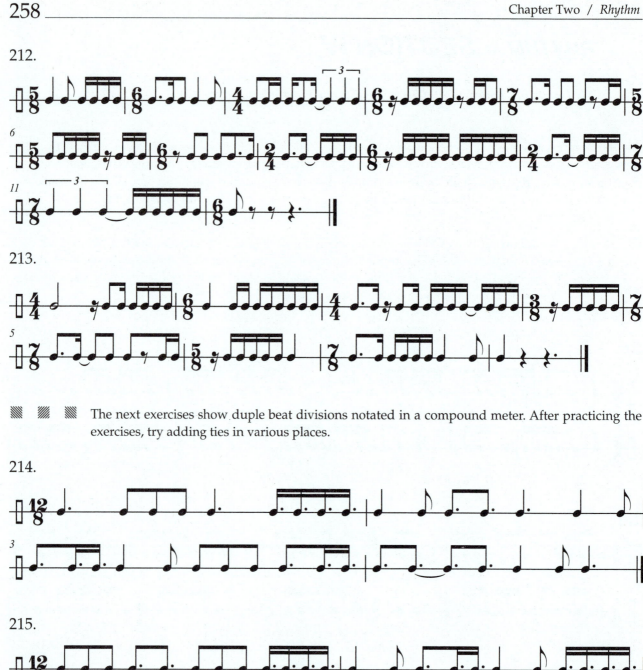

213.

The next exercises show duple beat divisions notated in a compound meter. After practicing the exercises, try adding ties in various places.

214.

215.

216.

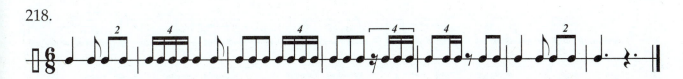 Here the duple divisions are shown in alternate notation. Many nineteenth-century scores represent duple divisions in a compound meter in this way. Modern scores tend to use the notation of the previous examples.

217.

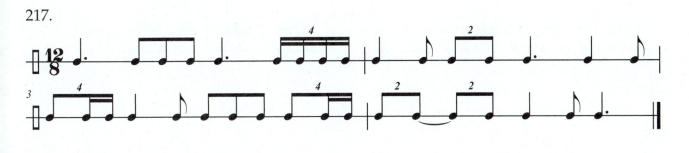

218.

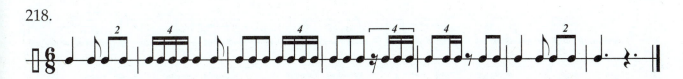

 When dividing a single beat into a quintuplet, focus on evenly dividing the pulse into five. You may find it helpful to think of a five-syllable word that replicates the sound of five evenly divided attacks. We recommend the words "navigational" for quintuplets and "circumnavigational" for septuplets. (You could also use "intellectual" and "pseudointellectual.") While it is certainly possible to devise word-rhythm associations for any possible rhythm, the use of this device seems more appropriate to the challenges of dividing a beat into five and seven.

219.

220.

221.

░ ▨ ▨ Try these exercises at a very slow tempo first, to hear the various divisions of the beat.

222.

223.

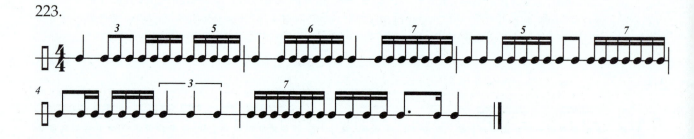

░ ▨ ▨ The next several rhythms explore new divisions and combinations. Try these at both very slow
and moderate tempi.

224.

▨ ▨ ▨   Metric modulation is a technique in which a rhythmic value suddenly bears a new relationship to the beat, thereby changing the tempo. In the next example, the quintuplet division starting in the first measure becomes the regular sixteenth note at the beginning of the fourth measure. This means that what had previously been 1/5 of a beat is now only 1/4 of a beat, and the tempo has increased from quarter = 80 to quarter = 100. In this example, find the common beat (the quintuplet), hear that rhythm in relation to the original tempo, and then shift to the new pulse at the new tempo's bar line.

230.

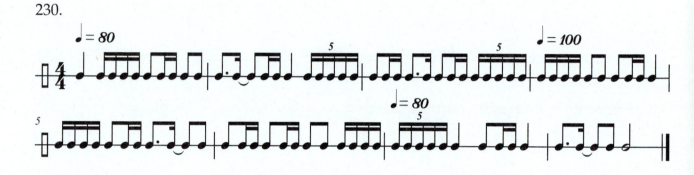

231.

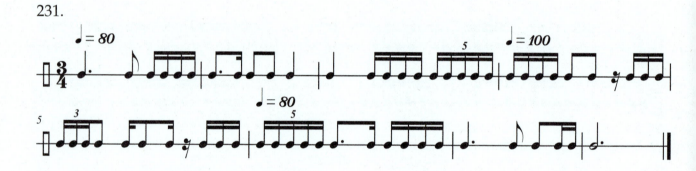

▨ ▨ ▨   In this exercise, the quarter note triplet has to become the quarter note in the fourth measure. Shift back at the sixth measure.

232.

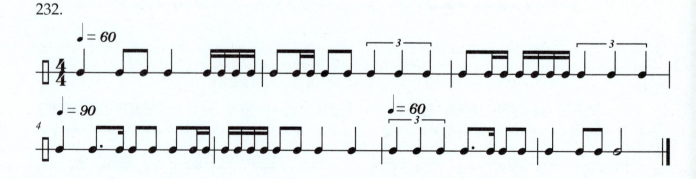

233.

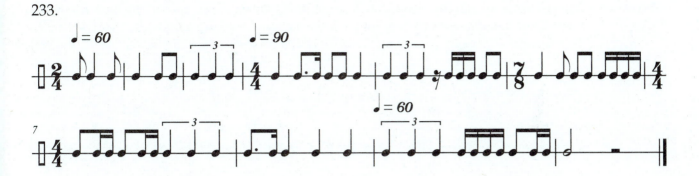

▨ ▨ ▨ Here the dotted eighth note becomes the quarter note, shifting the tempo from quarter = 60 to quarter = 80.

234.

235.

▨ ▨ ▨ The next exercise illustrates four against three and three against four. Try performing this in a number of ways: sing one line, tap the other; tap with two hands; sing with another student; etc. (Compare this with exercises 112 and 113, which illustrate two against three.)

236.

The next exercise shifts the tempo in a relationship of three to four. As you sing the rhythm, the attacks will sound like steady notes of the same duration, but the conducting pattern will relate to these notes differently, depending on which tempo is expressed.

237.

Here, the dotted eighth note becomes the quarter note. Which rhythm in measure 6 will sound the same as a rhythm in measure 4 or 5?

238.

Here, the septuplet becomes the sixteenth note, shifting the tempo from quarter = 60 to quarter = 105 and back.

239.

240.

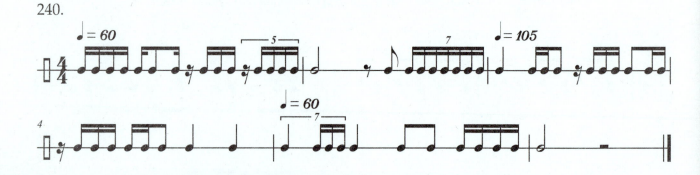

The next exercises incorporate rests and additional rhythms.

Try these additional subdivision exercises. Set a metronome to a tempo, and match the quarter note to the metronome.

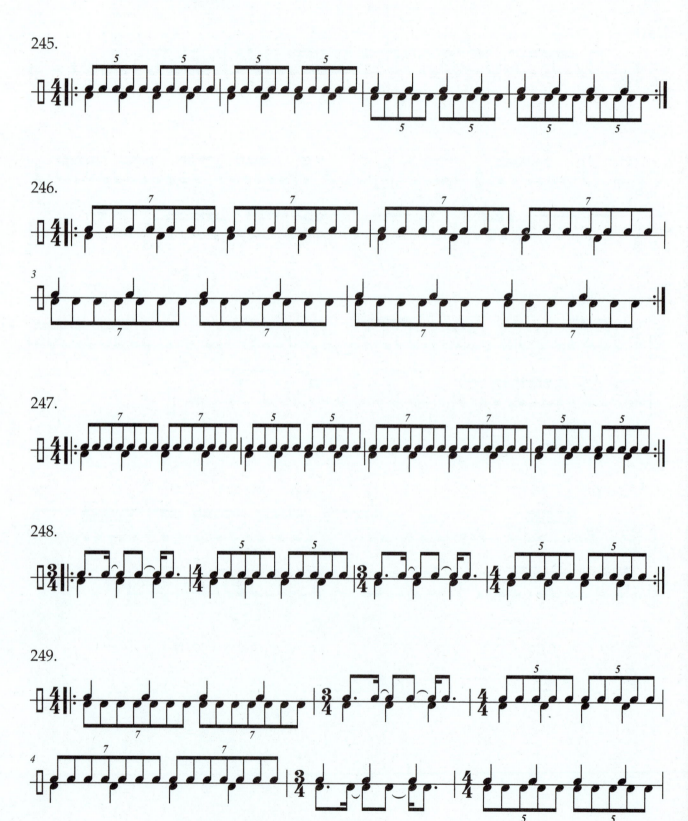

245.

246.

247.

248.

249.

▧ CHAPTER THREE ▧

Duets

The experience of singing one part while listening to another develops that sense of independence so essential to a good ensemble performer. Hearing the harmonic and contrapuntal relation between your melodic line and another will help maintain correct intonation and rhythmic precision. For additional practice, it is useful to play one part at the piano while singing the other. These duets may also be used for dictation.

DUETS ▨ SECTION I

To be used with Section I of all other chapters

The first five duets are restricted to consecutive scale steps.

1. *Flowing*

2. *Lento*

3. *Larghetto*

4. *Larghetto*

5. *Allegro*

6. *Con moto*

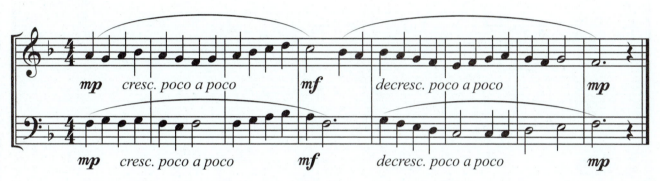

 Though comprised mostly of scale steps, the following four duets introduce intervallic skips of the third, fourth, and fifth.

7. *Andante*

8. *Allegretto*

9.   *Call and answer*

10.   *Gently*

The next two duets practice skips in the tonic triad.

11.   *Allegretto*

12.   *Andante*

13. *Moderato con moto*

▨ ▨ ▨ The next five duets are in the minor mode.

14. *Andante*

15. *Moderato con moto*

16. *Allegretto*

17. *Moderato*

18. *Moderato*

19. *Legato*

20. *Andante*

▨ ▨ ▨ The next three duets are in the minor mode.

21. *Andante cantabile*

22. *Larghetto*

23. *Adagietto*

▨ ▨ ▨

The next five duets introduce the alto clef.

24. *Allegro moderato*

25. *Allegretto*

26. *Allegro*

27. *Allegro con spirito*

28. *Moderato con moto*

29. *Allegro giocoso*

30. *Allegro*

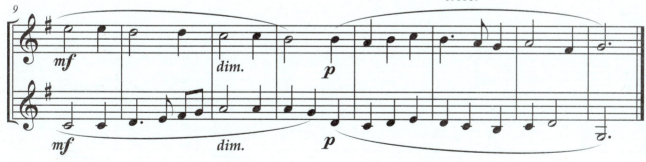

31. *Allegretto*

32. *Allegro moderato*

The next duet introduces syncopation.

33. *Semplice*

34. *Allegretto*

35. *Andante espressivo*

36. *Allegretto*

37. *Andante con moto*

38. *Fliessend*

DUETS ▨ SECTION II

To be used with Section II of all other chapters

39. *Andante con moto*

40. *Andantino*

41. *Andantino*

42. *Langsam*

43. *Lento*

44. *Andante espressivo*

45. *Mesto*

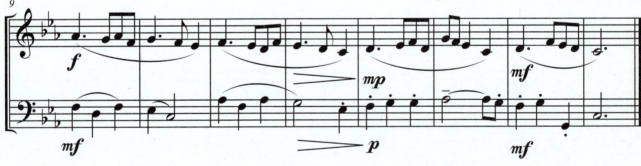

46. *Mässig*

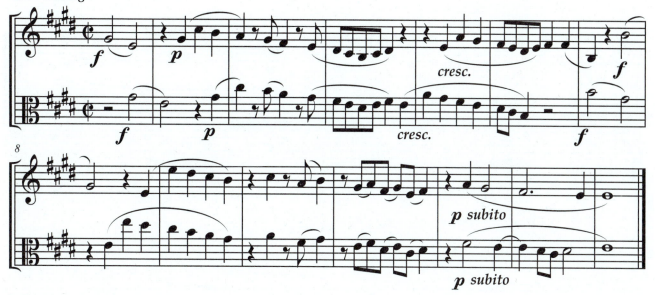

47. *Allegro con spirito*

 Tenor clef is introduced in this duet.

48. *Moderato*

(Continued)

48. **Moderato (Continued)**

49. **En allant**

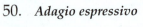

50. **Adagio espressivo**

51. *Andantino, con rubato*

52. *Andante cantabile*

53. *Allegretto giocoso*

54. *Smoky (Trio)*

55. *Allegretto*

56. *Allegro gioviale*

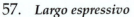 The next three duets contain chromatic neighbor tones.

57. *Largo espressivo*

58. *Giocoso*

59. *Andantino*

60. *Allegro*

61. *Con brio*

(Continued)

61. *Con brio (Continued)*

62. *Andante con moto*

The next nine duets contain pitches that suggest secondary dominants and tonicizations. Perform a harmonic analysis of these exercises to understand the key implications. Note, too, the chromatic passing tones in exercises 63–66.

63. *Mässig*

64. *Flowing*

65. *Andantino*

66. *Andante*

(Continued)

66. *Andante (Continued)*

67. *Andante cantabile*

68. *Rhythmically*

69. *Moderato*

70. **With a lilt**

71. *Allegretto*

The next eight duets are modal.

72. *Mesto* (transposed Dorian)

73. *Spiritoso* **(Dorian)**

74. *Andantino* **(Dorian)**

75. *Ben ritmico* **(Phrygian)**

76. *Berceuse* **(Phrygian)**

77. *Allegro* **(Mixolydian)**

78. *Grazioso e con moto* **(Phrygian)**

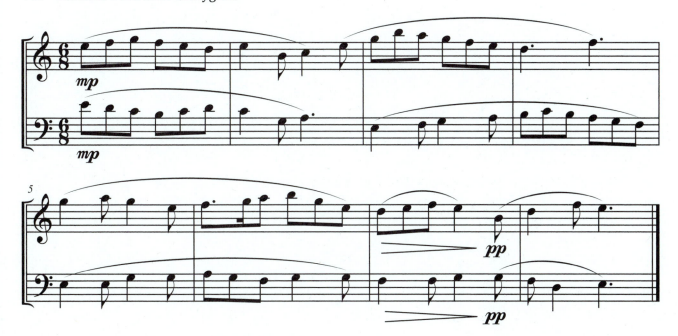

79. *Doucement* (Mixolydian)

To be used with Section III of all other chapters

The duets in Section III contain a variety of tonicizations. Be aware of the implied keys.

80. *Moderately fast*

81. *Modéré*

85. *Langsam*

86. *Andante con moto*

87. *Grazioso*

(Continued)

87. *Grazioso (Continued)*

88. *Moderato con tenerezza*

89. *Vif et gai*

90. *Lively*

91. *Lively, with humor*

92. *Moderato*

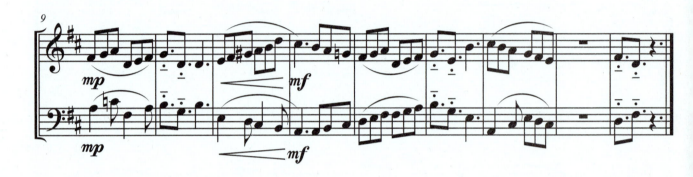

93. *Allegro moderato*

94. *Spiritoso*

95. *Allegretto*

(Continued)

95. *Allegretto (Continued)*

96. *Lebhaft*

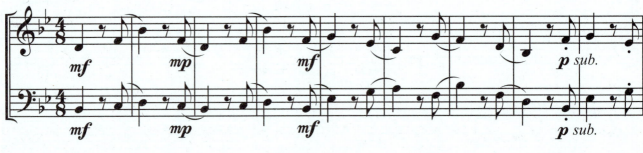

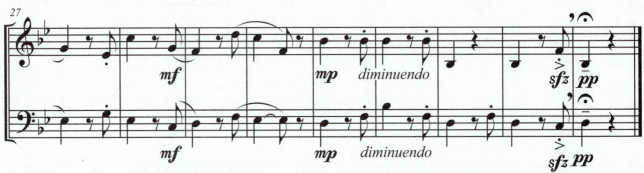

97. *Adagietto*

98. *Largo*

99. *Cheerful*

(Continued)

99. *Cheerful (Continued)*

100. *Lento*

101. *Cantabile*

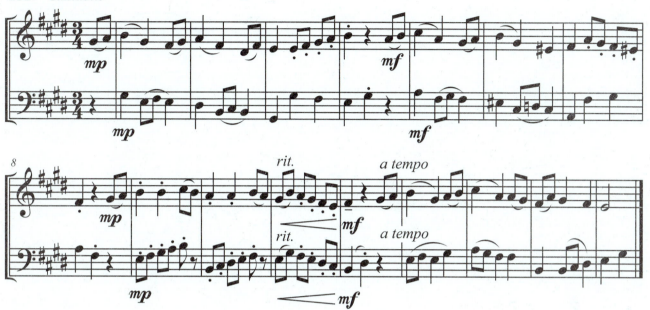

The next two duets contain the Neapolitan harmony. Do a harmonic analysis of the next two duets, identifying the Neapolitan chord.

102. *Marziale*

103. *Moderato*

104. *Andante affettuoso*

105. *Langsam und ausdrucksvoll*

106. *Con moto*

(Continued)

106. *Con moto (Continued)*

107. *Allegro molto*

108. *Adagietto, con espressione*

109. *Brisk*

110. *Scherzando*

111. *Vivo*

DUETS ▦ **SECTION IV**

To be used with Section IV of all other chapters

112. *Allegro deciso*

113. *Andante espressivo*

(Continued)

113. *Andante espressivo (Continued)*

114. *Mässig*

115. *Etwas langsam*

116. *Affettuoso*

117. *Allegro deciso*

118. *Merrily*

119. *Con brio*

120. *Adagietto*

121. *Andante*

122. *Ziemlich langsam*

123. *Andante con moto*

(Continued)

123.   *Andante con moto (Continued)*

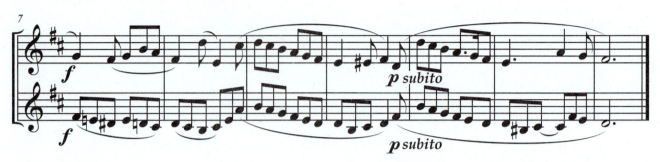

124.   *Gedehnt*

    The next duet contains a Neapolitan harmony.

125.   *Gioviale, ma andantino*

126. *Gemütlich*

127.   *Andante affetuoso*

128.   **With a lilt**

129. *Amabile*

130. *Bewegt*

131. *Doucement*

132. *Gedehnt*

(Continued)

132. *Gedehnt* (Continued)

▨ ▨ ▨ Analyze the following duet. Where are the augmented sixth chords? How does each function? Identify the Neapolitan chord.

133. *Grazioso*

The next six duets mix modes and keys, often simultaneously. In the next duet, the treble line is in D major, while the bass line is in D minor.

134. *Andante*

 In the next duet, both lines mix modes.

135. *Andante espressivo*

The treble line in the next duet implies the key of E major, while the bass line implies E Aeolian.

136. *Molto lento*

137. *Deciso*

138. *Allegretto e marcato*

The next duet is polytonal, the treble line in G major and the bass line in E♭ major

139. *March*

☰ CHAPTER FOUR ☰

Sing and Play

These exercises provide an introductory experience in singing with piano accompaniment. The great benefit of this kind of exercise is that it allows the sight singer to hear and demonstrate an understanding of coordinated rhythmic and harmonic relationships by a musical perfomance singing and playing at the same time. Of course, this models the best type of performance in so many ways: most music making involves coordinating more than one person and more than one line of music. The skills acquired singing melodies or rhythms are thus put into a "real" musical context with the duets and Sing and Play exercises.

These short pieces should be sung and played by the same person. Therefore, the piano parts have been kept simple, though they increase in difficulty. The emphasis is on the melodic line and its relationship to the accompaniment. If you have little expe-

rience with the piano, you may use the duets in Chapter Two as additional easy Sing and Play exercises. The piano can also be especially useful in overcoming difficulties with intonation. We suggest that a number of these exercises be studied each week prior to meeting in class.

Sing and Play exercises are especially valuable for giving harmonic context to the melodies you are singing. These exercises also help with intonation and general musicianship skills. In order to give you more time to work through these exercises, your instructor may ask you to record them outside of class and submit the recordings electronically.

Each section concludes with more challenging examples derived from the musical literature. Less experienced pianists may wish to play an even more simplified adaptation of the piano part.

SING AND PLAY ▩ SECTION I

To be used with Section I of all other chapters

▩ ▩ ▩ These first exercises include a piano part that utilizes a single clef and can be performed with one hand, but still provides the basic harmonic outline of the melody. Notice how the melodic line coordinates with the harmony in terms of chord tones and non-chord tones. Playing these harmonies along with the melodies will reinforce this connection and also help with intonation.

1. *Moderato*

2. *Andante*

▩ ▩ ▩ As an added challenge to the next example, try adding one note in the bass (left hand) that is the root of each triad.

3. *Moderato*

4. *Allegro*

5. *Andante*

 The next several exercises provide music for both the right hand and the left hand notated on a single staff. Play the lowest note with your left hand, and the upper three with your right.

6. *Allegro*

7. *Allegro*

Notice that the note in the left hand is not *always* the root of the triad.

8. *Andante sostenuto*

9a. *Largo*

 Now the same example is notated using a complete grand staff for the piano part. Try to "see" the entire harmony as outlined in the piano part as a single entity. If it is too challenging to play both clefs of the piano part, try singing the melody while playing only the right hand or the left hand of the piano part.

9b. *Largo*

The next two example have a single-line piano part. Note how the rhythms coordinate between the voice and piano.

10. *Andante*

11. *Allegro*

The next several examples have just one or two notes in the right hand part. Put those notes together with the left hand, and try to "see" the complete chord that is represented. Again, if playing two hands is too much of a challenge, play one hand while singing the exercise.

12a. *Allegro* **(maggiore)**

12b. *Allegro* **(minore)**

13. *Allegretto*

14. *Andante*

15. *Allegretto*

19. *Allegro*

20. *Moderato*

21. *Andante*

22a. *Andante* (maggiore)

22b. *Andante* (minore)

23a. *Andantino* (maggiore)

23b. *Andantino* (minore)

24. *Allegretto*

(Continued)

24. Allegretto (Continued)

25. Moderato

26. Allegro

27a. *Moderato* (**maggiore**)

27b. *Moderato* (**minore**)

28. *Allegretto*

29a. *Allegro* (**maggiore**)

29b. *Allegro* (**minore**)

The next example is a well-known spiritual. Once you have played the piece in the original key, try transposing it to other keys. When transposing the piano part, think of the entire chord, and also think of the chord tone that is in the bass, and the one that is in the soprano. The rest of the voicing should take care of itself. You could also experiment with improvising different voicings and rhythmic patterns of the piano part.

30. "Swing Low, Sweet Chariot"
    Slowly   *Traditional*

31. **"Non più andrai"**
    Vivace

Mozart: *Le nozze di Figaro*

32. *Larghetto*   **Handel:** *Messiah*

33.   **Smetana:** *The Moldau*

34.

Handel: *Messiah*

35. *Andante*

Fauré: *Pavane*

36. *Stately*

Purcell: *Trumpet Tune*

SING AND PLAY ▨ SECTION II

To be used with Section II of all other chapters

▨ ▨ ▨ These exercises explore a variety of combinations of clefs, giving students experience that is similar to score reading. Always look at the various combinations to "see" the harmony that results. Try to see the whole as an integrated musical unit.

This section also introduces a broader range of some simple pianistic figuration. Notice how the piano figuration "adds up" to familiar harmonies. Many of these piano parts will also benefit from use of the sustain pedal.

As with all Sing and Play exercises, classes may find benefits from recording performances which can be uploaded to SoundCloud, YouTube, Google Classroom, or another learning management system. In this way, students can get the benefits of studying these exercises without using class time.

37. *Moderato*

38. *Andantino*

39. *Allegro*

40. *Andantino*

41. *Lento*

▨ ▨ ▨   If the piano figuration in these exercises presents too great a challenge, try reducing the right
hand to "block chords."

42.   *Allegretto*

43.   *Allegretto*

44. *Andantino*

con pedale

45a. *Moderato* **(maggiore)**

45b. *Moderato* (minore)

46. *Andante*

47a. *Modéré* **(maggiore)**

47b. *Modéré* **(minore)**

▨ ▨ ▨ The next example is challenging because of the independent rhythms in each part.

48. *Allegro*

49a. *Moderato* (**maggiore**)

49b. *Moderato* **(minore)**

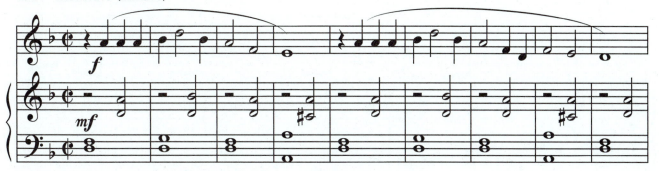

▨ ▨ ▨   This Sing and Play is like a string quartet reduced to three clefs. Sing the viola part and play the other voices.

50. *Allegro*

51. *Lento*

52. *Lento*

53. *Allegro*

54a. *Andantino* (**maggiore**)

54b.   *Andantino* **(minore)**

55.   *Andante*

56. *Allegretto*

57. *Lento*

(Continued)

57. *Lento (Continued)*

58. *Allegro ma non troppo*

59. *Andante*

60. *Adagio*

61. *Allegro*

62. *Langsam*

63. *Andante*

64. *Moderato*

65. *Adagio*

66. *Andante cantabile*

67. *Allegretto*

68. *Adagietto*

69. *Allegro moderato*   **Schubert: Symphony No. 8, I**

70. *Andante*   **Brahms: Symphony No. 3, Op. 90, II**

71. *Slowly*   **Ravel:** *Pavane pour une infante défunte*

72.   *Allegro brilliante*   **Verdi:** *La Traviata, Act II*

73. *Moderato* Tchaikovsky: *Swan Lake*

74.   *Allegro, vivace e con brio*   **Beethoven: Symphony No. 8, I**

75. *Schnell*

Schubert: *Erlkönig*

SING AND PLAY ▨ *SECTION III*

To be used with Section III of all other chapters

76a. *Allegro assai* **(maggiore)**

76b. *Allegro assai* **(minore)**

77. *Allegretto*

(Continued)

77. **Allegretto** (Continued)

78. **Lento**

79. **Andantino**

80. *Andante con moto*

81. *Allegretto grazioso*

82. *Largo*

83. *Allegretto*

84a. *Moderato* (maggiore)

84b. *Moderato* **(minore)**

85. *Pastorale*

(Continued)

85. Pastorale (Continued)

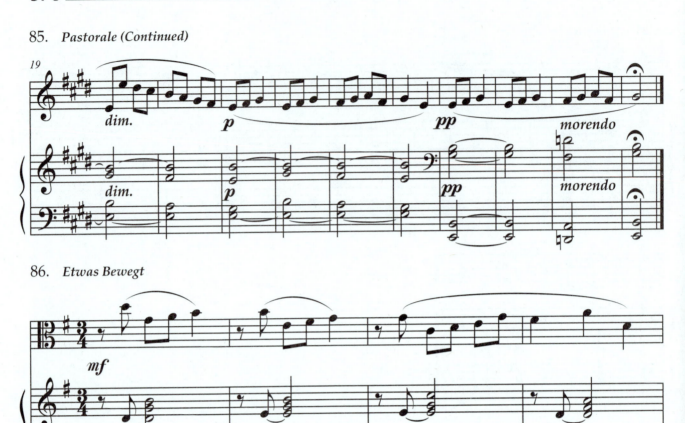

86. Etwas Bewegt

87. Mässig und zart

88. *Andantino*

Appoggiatura: see *Glossary*.

89. *Langsam*

This next example features familiar jazz harmonies. The chords notated in the piano part are represented by their standard chord symbols. Notice how each note of the piano part is represented in the chord symbol. Try improvising a more elaborate piano part by arpeggiating the notes of each chord.

90. *Slowly*

91. *Larghetto*

(Continued)

91. *Larghetto (Continued)*

◼ ▨ ◼ The next two examples demonstrate motion to V and the relative major.

92. *Berceuse*

93. *Mässig und ausdrucksvoll*

Notice the use of mixture and applied V^7 and vii^7 in the following examples.

94. *Andante maestoso*

(Continued)

94. *Andante maestoso (Continued)*

▨ ▨ ▨ What is the function of the harmony in m. 13?

95. *Andante cantabile*

96. *Recitativo*

Two Chorales: These two famous chorales are from the *Choralbuch* of Alfred Dörffel. These are not the traditional Bach harmonizations, but we present these very familiar chorales in easy arrangements for an introduction to chorale playing, itself a good introduction to score reading. You will notice that the tenor voice "moves" from treble to bass clef, depending on whether it should be played by the right or the left hand. Try playing three voices and singing either the tenor or alto part.

97. **"Lobe den Herren, den mächtigen König"**

98.   "Vom Himmel hoch, da komm ich her"   Martin Luther, 1538

99.   *Allegro*   Beethoven: Symphony No. 5, IV

(Continued)

99. *Allegro (Continued)*

100. *Allegretto*

Beethoven: Symphony No. 7, II

Sing one of the upper voices and play the other two.

101.

J. S. Bach: French Suite No. 1, Menuet II

(Continued)

101. *(Continued)*

▨ ▨ ▨ Sing the upper line and play the lower. (Some registers have been altered.)

102.   *Recht gemächlich* ♩. = 54   **Mahler: Symphony No.1, II (Trio)**

103.   **Verdi:** *La Traviata, Act II*

SING AND PLAY ▓ *SECTION IV*

To be used with Section IV of all other chapters

104. *Innig*

105. *Andante sostenuto*

con pedale

106.   *Mit Empfindung*

(Continued)

106. *Mit Empfindung (Continued)*

107. *Tempo di valzer*

108. *Andante con moto*

109. *Ziemlich langsam*

(Continued)

109. *Ziemlich langsam (Continued)*

110. *Slowly* ♩ = 72

111. *Andantino con grazia*

112. *Allegro con brio*

(Continued)

112. *Allegro con brio (Continued)*

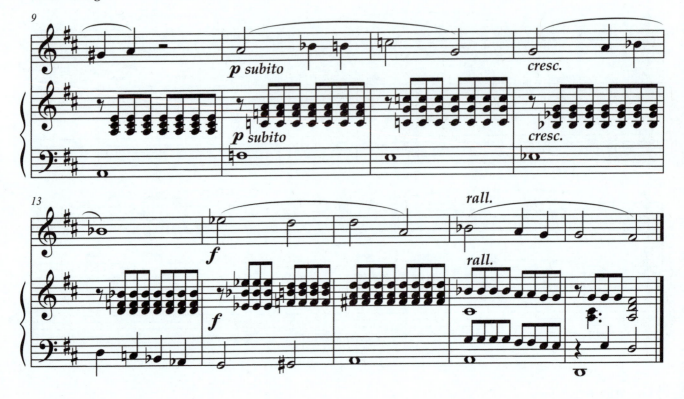

113. *Pensive* ♩ = 66

114. *Moderate*

115. *Slow*

116. *Tenderly*

117. *Moderately slow*

118. *Slowly*

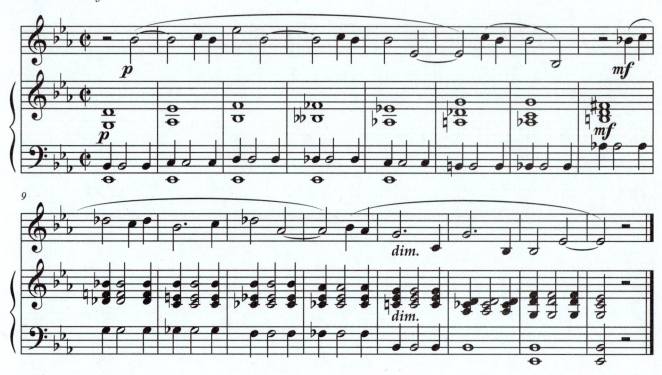

119. *Slow and expressive*

In the next three examples, the melody consists only of whole steps, half steps and perfect fourths, similar to the melodies found in Chapter 1, Section V, Part 2.

120. *Molto sostenuto*

121. *Modéré*

122. *Lentement*

Sing the violin 1 part and play the lower two staves.

123. *Sehr langsam*   **Mozart: Symphony No. 35, Trio**

124.

Tchaikovsky: Violin Concerto, Op. 35, I

(Continued)

124. *(Continued)*

125. *Sehr langsam*   **Schubert:** *Ave Maria*

126. *Andante, un poco adagio*

Brahms: Sonata No. 1 for Clarinet (Viola)
and Piano in F minor, Op. 120, II

127. *Mässig*   **Schubert:** *Ständchen*

128. **"Wie Melodien zieht es mir"**   **Brahms: Op. 105, No. 1**
                                                               Text: Klaus Groth

Wie Me - lo - di - en___ zieht es mir lei - se durch den Sinn, wie

Früh - lings blu - men blüht es und schwebt wie Duft da - hin   und

schwebt wie Duft da - hin   Doch kommt das Wort___ und___ fasst es und

führt es vor das Aug, wie Ne - bel-grau er - blasst es und schwin-det wie ein

Hauch, und schwin-det wie ein Hauch, Und den noch

ruht im Rei - me ver - bor-gen wohl ein Duft, den mild aus stil-lem Kei - me ein

(Continued)

128. **"Wie Melodien zieht es mir"** *(Continued)*

Supplementary Exercises

These drills are designed to focus on various technical problems. Part I is concerned principally with the development of the sense of key. Part II concentrates on problems involving chromaticism. Both parts also contain rhythmic patterns arranged in order of increasing complexity. Learn each exercise slowly and accurately, then increase the speed as much as possible.

SUPPLEMENTARY EXERCISES ▨ *PART I*

For use with Sections I and II of all other chapters

▨ ▨ ▨ The first nine exercises focus on major scales and triads.

7.

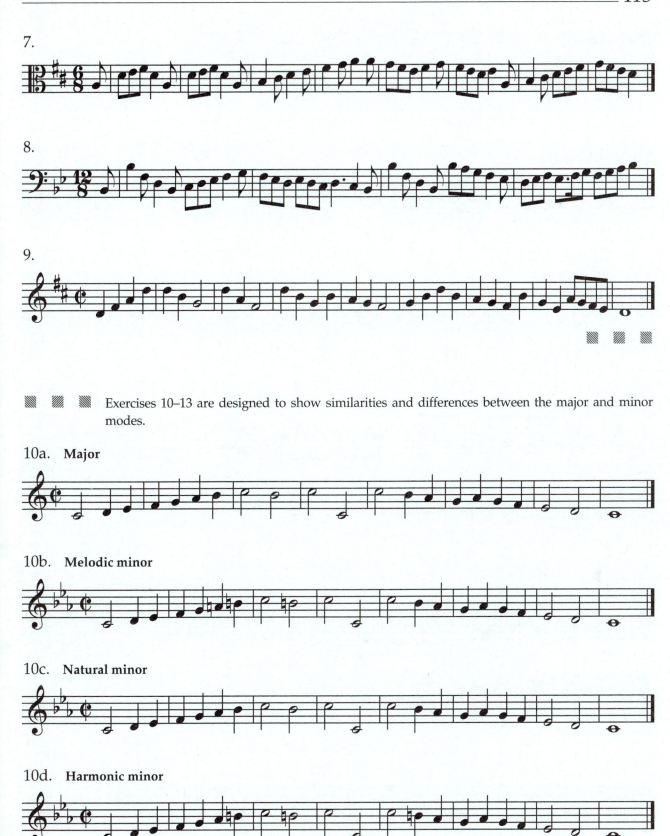

8.

9.

Exercises 10–13 are designed to show similarities and differences between the major and minor modes.

10a.   Major

10b.   Melodic minor

10c.   Natural minor

10d.   Harmonic minor

11a.   Major

11b.   Melodic minor

11c.   Natural minor

12a.

12b.

13a.

13b.

The next seven melodies focus on scales and triads in the minor mode.

14.

15.

11

16.

17.

9

18.

19.

20.

21.

22.

simile

23.

9

24.

9

31.

32.

33.

34.

35.

36.

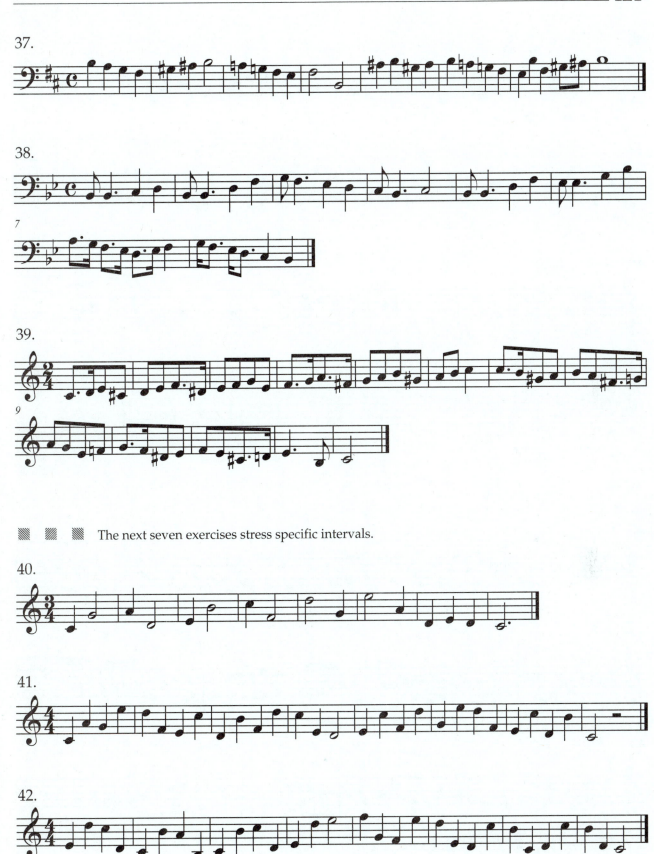

The next seven exercises stress specific intervals.

50.

51.

52.

53.

54.

55.

56.

4

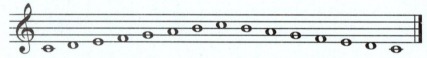

57. Ionian mode (major scale)

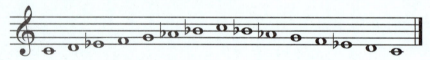

58. Aeolian mode (natural minor scale)

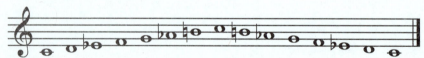

59. Harmonic minor scale

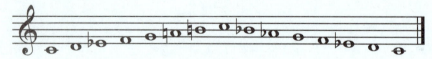

60. Melodic minor scale

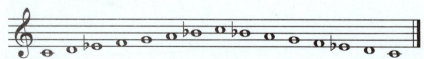

61. Dorian mode

62. **Mixolydian mode**

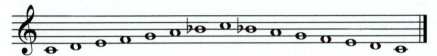

63. **Phrygian mode**

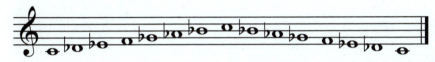

64. **Locrian mode**

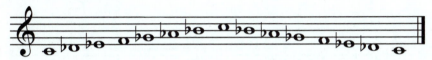

65. **Lydian mode**

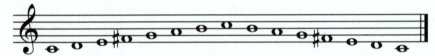

SUPPLEMENTARY EXERCISES ▨ *PART II*

For use with Sections III and IV of all other chapters

▨ ▨ ▨ Various scales and modes for practice.

66. Whole-tone scale

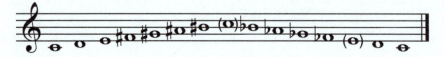

67. Chromatic scale

68a. Whole-tone and chromatic scale

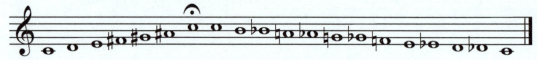

68b. Chromatic and whole-tone scale

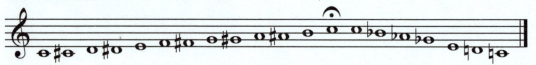

69.

70.

71.

72.

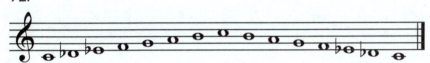

 Octatonic scales have eight notes arranged in a pattern of alternating whole steps and half steps. Three octatonic scales:

73.

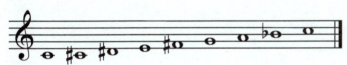

74.

75.

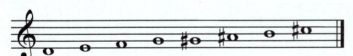

 The remaining exercises are studies in chromaticism.

76.

77.

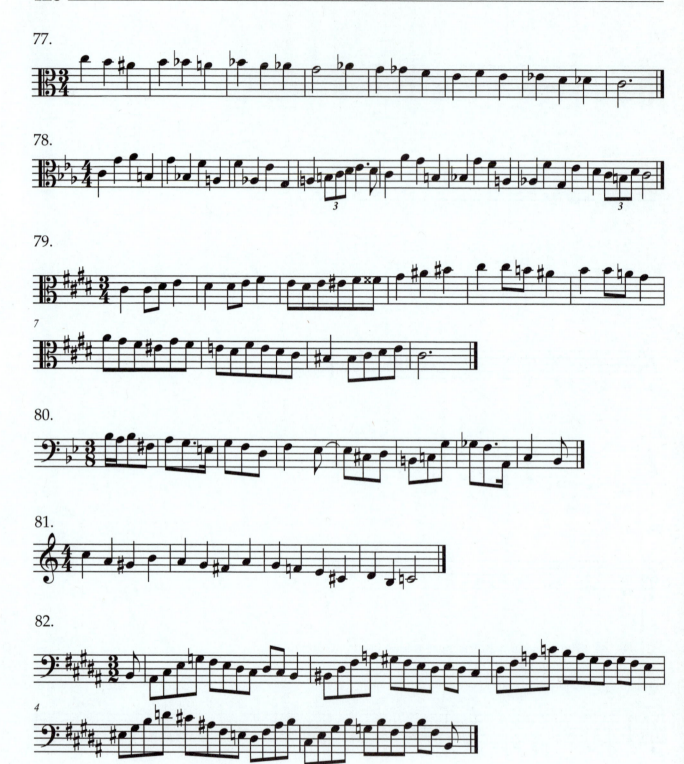

83.

84.

11

85.

13

Glossary of Musical Terms

All terms are Italian unless otherwise noted. Abbreviations are given in parentheses.

Accelerando (accel.), gradually getting faster

Acciaccatura, a short appoggiatura

Adagietto, somewhat faster than adagio

Adagio, slow (slower than andante, faster than largo)

Affetto, tenderness

Affettuoso, tender

Affretando, pressing forward

Agitato, agitated

Al fine, to the end

Alla, to the, at the, in the style of

Allargando, getting slower (crescendo often implied)

Allegretto, moderately fast (slower than allegro, faster than andante)

Allegro, fast, cheerful

All'ottava (8va), at the octave

Amabile, with love

Andante, moderately slow (slower than allegretto, faster than adagio)

Andantino, in modern usage, somewhat faster than andante; in older usage, somewhat slower than andante

Anima, spirit

Animato, animated, spirited

Animé, Fr., animated, spirited

A piacere, rhythm and tempo played at performer's discretion; freely

Appassionato, impassioned, intense

Appoggiatura, a melodic ornament; of the many types there are two main classifications: the *accented (long) appoggiatura* and the *short appoggiatura* (grace note). The first, written as a small note, is accented and borrows time value from the note it precedes. See note on page 377. The second is usually written as a small eighth or sixteenth note with a slanting stroke through the flag and stem. It is executed quickly, so that the accent falls on the melody note it precedes.

Arietta, a small aria

Assai, very

Assez, Fr., fairly, enough

A tempo, at the original speed

Attacca, attack or begin what follows without pause

Ausdrucksvoll, Ger., expressive

Avec, Fr., with

Ballando, dancing

Barcarolle, Fr., gently rocking

Ben, well, very

Berceuse, Fr., lullaby

Bewegt, Ger., rather fast, agitated

Breit, Ger., broad, stately

Brillante, brilliant, sparkling

Brio, sprightliness, spirit

Calando, decreasing in both dynamics and tempo

Calma, Calmo, calm, tranquil

Calme, Fr., calm

Calore, warmth, passion

Cantabile, in a singing or vocal style

Cedez, Fr., slow down

Colla voce, literally "with the voice," meaning that the accompanist should follow the free rhythm used by the singer

Comodo, at a leisurely, convenient pace

Con, with

Corta, short

Crescendo (cresc.), increasing in volume of sound

Da capo (D. C.), from the beginning

Da capo al fine, repeat from the beginning to the end; that is, to the place where *fine* is written

Dal segno al fine, repeat from the sign to the end; that is, to the place where *fine* is written

Deciso, decisive, bold

Decrescendo (decresc.), decreasing in volume of sound

Del, of the

Deliberatamente, deliberately

Détaché, Fr., detached

Di, of

Diminuendo (dim.), decreasing in volume of sound

Doch, Ger., yet

Dolce, sweet (*soft* is also implied)

Dolcissimo, very sweet

Dolente, Fr., sorrowfully, plaintively

Doloroso, sorrowfully

Doux, Fr., sweet (*soft* is also implied)

Doucement, Fr., sweet (*soft* is also implied)

Drammatico, dramatically

E, ed, and

Eco, echo

Einfach, Ger., simple

Empfindung, Ger., expression

En allant, Fr., moving, flowing

Energico, energetic

Eroica, heroically

Espressione, expression

Espressivo (espr.), expressive

Et, Fr., and

Etwas, Ger., somewhat

Expressif, Fr., expressive

Fastoso, stately, pompous

Feierlich, Ger., solemn

Feurig, Ger., fiery, impetuous

Fine, end

Fliessend, Ger., flowing

Force, Fr., strength, force

Forte (f), loud

Fortissimo (ff), very loud

Forza, force

Frisch, Ger., brisk, lively

Fröhlich, Ger., joyous, gay

Funèbre, funereal

Fuoco, fire, fiery

Gai, Fr., gay

Gaio, gay

Galop, Fr., a lively round-dance in duple meter

Gavotte, Fr., a French dance generally in common time, strongly accented, beginning on the third beat

Gedehnt, Ger., extended, sustained

Gemütlich, Ger., relaxed

Geschwind, Ger., quick

Getragen, Ger., sustained

Gigue, Fr., a very fast dance of English origin in triple or sextuple meter

Giocoso, playful

Gioviale, jovial

Giusto, exact

Gracieux, Fr., graceful

Grave, very slow, solemn (generally indicates the slowest tempo)

Grazia, grace

Grazioso, graceful

Gustoso, happy and forcefully

Il più, the most

Im Zeitmass, Ger., in the original speed

Innig, Ger., heartfelt, ardent

Innocente, unaffected, artless

Kraft, Ger., strength

Kräftig, Ger., strong, robust

La, It. and Fr., the

Ländler, Ger., a country dance in triple meter

Langsam, Ger., slow

Larghetto, not as slow as largo

Largo, slow, broad

Lebendig, Ger., lively

Lebhaft, Ger., lively, animated

Legato, to be performed with no interruption between tones; in a smooth and connected manner

Léger, Fr., light

Leggiero (also Leggero), light, delicate

Leise, Ger., soft

Lent, Fr., slow

Lentement, Fr., slowly

Lento, slow; not as slow as adagio

Lieblich, Ger., lovely

L'istesso tempo, in the same tempo as the previous section

Lugubre, mournful

Lunatico, performed in the spirit of lunacy

Lusingando, coaxingly

Lustig, Ger., cheerful

Ma, but

Maestoso, majestic, dignified

Maggiore, major (referring to mode)

Mais, Fr., but

Marcato, marked, with emphasis

Marcia, march

Marziale, martial

Mässig, Ger., moderate tempo

Mazurka, Polish national dance in triple meter

Meno, less

Menuetto, minuet (moderately slow dance in triple meter)

Mesto, sad, mournful

Mezza voce, with half voice, restrained

Mezzo forte (*mf*), moderately loud

Mezzo piano (*mp*), moderately soft

Minore, minor (referring to mode)

Minuetto, minuet (moderately slow dance in triple meter)

Misterioso, mysterious

Mit, Ger., with

Moderato, moderate (slower than allegro, faster than andante)

Modéré, Fr., moderate (slower than allegro, faster than andante)

Möglich, Ger., possible

Molto, much, very

Morendo, dying away

Mosso, in motion (*più mosso*, faster; *meno mosso*, slower)

Moto, motion

Mouvement, Fr., motion, tempo, movement

Munter, Ger., lively

Nicht, Ger., not

Niente, nothing

Non, not

Ongarese, Hungarian

Parlando, as though speaking or reciting

Pas, Fr., not

Pastorale, pastoral

Pedale, sustaining pedal on a piano

Perdendosi, gradually fading away

Pesante, heavy, ponderous

Peu, Fr., little

Piacere, at pleasure; expression is left to the performer's discretion

Piacevole, pleasant, graceful

Piano (*p*), soft

Pianissimo (*pp*), very soft

Più, more

Plus, Fr., more

Poco, little

Poco a poco, little by little, gradually

Polaca, in the manner of a Polonaise (Polish dance)

Pomposo, pompous

Portamento, a smooth gliding from one note to another

Possibile, possible

Pressez, Fr., press forward

Presto, very fast (faster than allegro)

Quasi, almost, nearly

Rallentando (*rall.*), gradually growing slower

Rasch, Ger., fast

Recitativo, sung in a declamatory manner

Retenu, Fr., held back

Rigore, strictness

Rigueur, Fr., strictness

Risoluto, firm, resolute

Ritardando (*rit.*), gradually growing slower

Ritenuto (*riten.*), held back

Ritmico, rhythmically

Rubato, literally, stolen; the term indicates freedom and flexibility of tempo so that the requirements of musical expression can be met

Ruhig, Ger., calm, tranquil

Saltarello, a lively dance of Italian origin, often in $\frac{9}{8}$

Sans, Fr., without

Scherzando, light, playful

Scherzo, a fast piece in triple meter

Scherzoso, jesting, playful

Schnell, Ger., fast

Seconda, second

Sehr, Ger., very

Semplice, simple, unaffected

Sempre, always

Sentimentale, It. and Fr., with sentiment

Senza fretta, without haste

Sforzando (*sf*, *sfz*), with force, accented

Siciliano, a moderately slow dance of pastoral character in $\frac{12}{8}$ or $\frac{6}{8}$ time

Simile, alike, in like manner

Smorzando, dying away

So, Ger., as

Sostenuto, sustained

Sotto voce, softly, with subdued voice

Spirito, spirit

Spiritoso, with spirit, animated

Staccato, detached

Stark, Ger., strong, vigorous

Stringendo, pressing forward

Subito (sub.), suddenly

Tanto, as much

Tarantella, a lively dance of Italian origin, usually in ⁶⁄₈

Tempo, time; refers to rate of motion

Tempo primo (Tempo I), in the original speed

Teneramente, tenderly, delicately

Tenerezza, tenderness

Tranquillo, tranquil

Très, Fr., very

Triste, It. and Fr., sad

Trop, Fr., too much, too

Troppo, too much, too

Un, It. and Fr., a

Und, Ger., and

Valse, Fr., waltz

Valzer, Ger., waltz

Vif, Fr., lively

Vite, Fr., quickly

Vivace, lively, quick

Vivement, Fr., lively

Vivo, lively, animated

Volta, turn or time

Walzer, Ger., waltz

Wie, Ger., as

Zart, Ger., tender, soft

Zeitmass, Ger., tempo

Ziemlich, Ger., somewhat, rather

Zu, Ger., too, to, by

Zuvor, Ger., previously

Zurückhalten, Ger., to hold back, to retard

Some Frequently Used Musical Signs

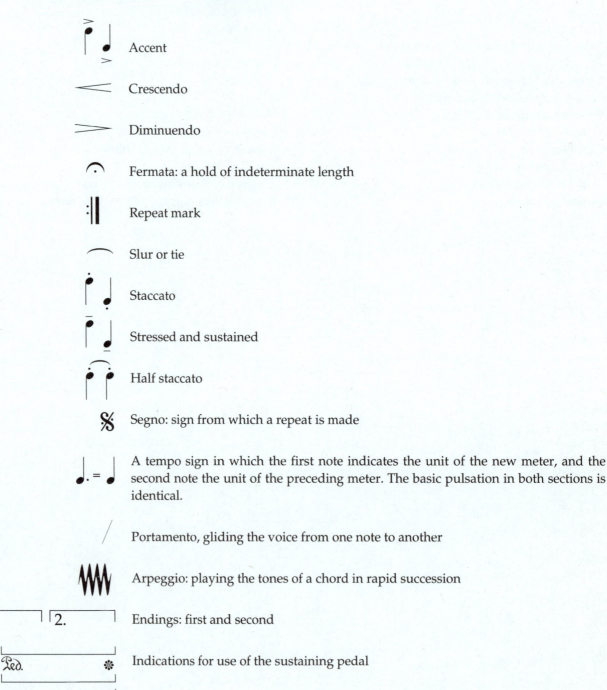

Accent

Crescendo

Diminuendo

Fermata: a hold of indeterminate length

Repeat mark

Slur or tie

Staccato

Stressed and sustained

Half staccato

Segno: sign from which a repeat is made

A tempo sign in which the first note indicates the unit of the new meter, and the second note the unit of the preceding meter. The basic pulsation in both sections is identical.

Portamento, gliding the voice from one note to another

Arpeggio: playing the tones of a chord in rapid succession

Endings: first and second

Indications for use of the sustaining pedal

Credits

Index

The index identifies the exercise number of the first occurrence of a topic in relevant chapters as well as significant examples of the topic thereafter.